Twins, Triplets, and More

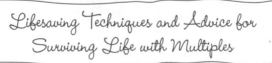

*Lifesaving Techniques and Advice for
Surviving Life with Multiples*

Pamela Fierro

Adamsmedia

Avon, Massachusetts

Published by Adams Media, an F+W Publications Company
57 Littlefield Street
Avon, MA 02322
www.adamsmedia.com

ISBN-10: 1-59869-688-2
ISBN-13: 978-1-59869-688-2

Printed in Canada.
J I H G F E D C B A

Library of Congress Cataloging-in-Publication Data
Fierro, Pamela.
Mommy rescue guide : twins, triplets, and more / Pamela Fierro.
p.   cm.
Includes bibliographical references.
ISBN-13: 978-1-59869-688-2 (spiral bound)
ISBN-10: 1-59869-688-2 (spiral bound)
1. Multiple birth—Popular works.
2. Multiple pregnancy—Popular works. I. Title.
RG696.F543 2007
618.2'5—dc22
2007039183

This publication is designed to provide accurate and authoritative
information with regard to the subject matter covered. It is sold
with the understanding that the publisher is not engaged in render-
ing legal, accounting, or other professional advice. If legal advice
or other expert assistance is required, the services of a competent
professional person should be sought.
— From a *Declaration of Principles* jointly adopted by a
Committee of the American Bar Association and
a Committee of Publishers and Associations

Many of the designations used by manufacturers and sellers to
distinguish their product are claimed as trademarks. Where those
designations appear in this book and Adams Media was aware of
a trademark claim, the designations have been printed with initial
capital letters.

This book is available at quantity discounts for bulk purchases.
For information, please call 1-800-289-0963.

Mommy Rescue Guide

Welcome to the lifesaving *Mommy Rescue Guide* series! Each *Mommy Rescue Guide* offers techniques and advice written by recognized parenting authorities.

These engaging, informative books give you the help you need when you need it the most! The *Mommy Rescue Guides* are quick, issue-specific, and easy to carry anywhere and everywhere.

You can read one from cover to cover or just pick out the information you need for rapid relief! Whether you're in a bind or you have some time, these books will make being a mom painless and fun!

Being a good mom has never been easier!

*This book is dedicated to Lauren and to Meredith,
for all the double delight they have brought to my life.
Because of them, I am able to write these words.*

Contents

Introduction

"I'M HAVING WHAT?!" Finding out that you are expecting more than one baby is a shock quite unlike any other. Your mind whirls with questions . . . "How did this happen?" "What does this mean?" "How will we manage?" "How much will it cost?"

Fortunately, this book will give you some answers. It will help you untangle the facts from the fiction, evaluate your options, and make informed decisions at every turn. From the potential pitfalls of a multiple pregnancy to the chaos of caring for numerous newborns, *Mommy Rescue Guide: Twins, Triplets, and More* has the advice you are seeking.

You'll discover what's really different about twins and multiples, how their birth will impact your lifestyle, and ways to cope with the challenges they create. You can rely on it for honest, accurate information delivered with compassion and care. Some of what you read may be alarming, but most will be reassuring. Having multiples is only half as bad as your worst fears, and twice as wonderful as you can possibly imagine!

Although the birth rate for twins and multiples has risen dramatically in recent years, they remain a fairly rare phenomenon. Most people know someone who is a twin, or perhaps they've seen media coverage of incredible families with extreme multiples. But only about 3 percent of the millions of women who give birth every year will have the privilege of being a mother of multiples. You're about to join an exclusive club!

It is my hope that you will relish your experience as a mother of multiples as much as I do, enjoying the opportunity to parent two children who share so much yet are so uniquely individual. It is a privilege to be an observer of their fascinating world and watch their bond develop and deepen as they grow up.

Chapter 1

An Introduction: What's Different About Multiples

WELCOME TO THE WONDERFUL world of multiples! If you just recently made the discovery that your family is being expanded by twins, triplets, or more, you are probably feeling a bit overwhelmed. You may be feeling a bunch of different emotions and this is normal! You may be curious as to how it came to pass. You may be anxious about how multiples will mesh with your family's lifestyle, and how you will meet the needs of several simultaneous siblings. Having multiples is a truly unique parenting experience, filled with fascination and occasional moments of frustration. Let's take a look at what sets you and your multiples apart.

You Are in a Special Class of Parents

By having twins, triplets, or other multiples, you have been granted inclusion into a special class of parents. Although they wouldn't necessarily have asked for this honor, most parents wouldn't trade it for the world. Maybe you have always had a secret fascination with multiples and suspected you would bear them. Or maybe you thought you'd be the last person on earth to have multiples. Either way, this blessing will set you apart from other families and bring a new designation to your identity as a parent.

Having multiples is extraordinary. If you gathered a group of one hundred parents, only two or three would be able to claim multiples. For the rest of your life, you are guaranteed to get a reaction when you talk about your children. Gasps of "Oh!" "Wow!" "Lucky you!" and "Better you than me!" are common responses when you tell someone you have multiples.

Some people might wonder what the big deal is about twins and multiples. Plenty of families have lots of kids, right? What makes it so different to have a few of them at once? There are many ways that having two, three, or more babies at the same time is different from having the same number of singletons. In some ways it makes family life easier, but in others it makes things much more complicated. No matter how close in age singletons may be, the fact remains

Mommy Knows Best

You'll often hear people say, "Oh, my kids were only eleven months apart. It was just like having twins." There's no easy way—and no good reason—to politely explain to someone that the two situations are nothing alike. It's easiest just to smile and nod agreeably.

that they were born one at a time. Their parents had at least nine months to prepare for the arrival of the next child. The organizational challenges of simultaneously meeting the needs of multiple newborns are simply more demanding.

The Impact of Birth Order

Birth order has a tremendous impact on the structure of families. Not only does it contribute to the personality development of each individual child, but it also sets the standard for how each child is treated. Older children have more freedom, but likewise more responsibility, because their advanced age makes them developmentally capable of handling it. Younger children benefit from interaction with their older siblings.

Multiples, on the other hand, lack the defined roles created by birth order. Being the same age, and generally of equal status within the family, there is no formalized structure for establishing order. The effort to create and reinvent a pecking order can generate ongoing tension for the family as the parents seek to intervene.

The Group Dynamic

Outsiders may look at your duo, trio, or higher order multiples and see two, three, or more kids. What they don't realize is that in addition to having these individual children, parents of multiples also have to contend with a group dynamic. With multiples, parents don't simply have an extra child or two.

The group dynamic adds an entirely new element. You know the old saying, "Two heads are better than one?" Working in conjunction with each other, a group of multiples is easily more daring, more creative, and more clever than any individual child on his or her own.

The companionship and cooperation of their same-age siblings often incites behavior that exceeds an individual child's limits. Together, multiples will invent more schemes, attempt more stunts, and create more messes. There is power in numbers, and managing that power is one of the biggest challenges that parents of multiples face.

Playing Fair

Another unique challenge is maintaining equality among multiples. It's often a struggle for parents of twins or more to ensure that each child gets his or her fair share; whether it is time, attention, or material goods, it is difficult (if not impossible) to always dole out an equitable portion. Life is simply not fair. Unfortunately, you can't convince multiples of that fact, and as a parent you can never quit striving to make it so! Soothing jealousy and stifling competition

Mindful Mommy

Some parents of multiples find it a challenge to teach their children principles of accountability because the twins, triplets, or more are accustomed to sharing joint responsibility with their co-multiples. Frequently rewarded and disciplined as a group, they share blame, as well as credit, without individual accountability.

is a constant battle for parents until multiples mature to an age where they can accept and appreciate the differences among them.

The Unique Bond Your Babies Have

The bond between a set of multiples is unique. Beginning even before birth, it is one of the longest and most enduring interpersonal relationships that a human being can have. It surpasses that of regular siblings. The intensity of this relationship often makes multiples the best of friends one moment and bitter enemies the next.

As a parent, you'll have a unique opportunity to watch your multiples' bond grow and develop from the very beginning. You'll have responsibility for nurturing each child as an individual within the context of their unique relationship to their co-multiples. It's never too early to start thinking about how you'll accomplish that balance.

Share and Share Alike

All members of a family have to learn to share to get along. But multiples share more than most siblings. Beginning in the womb, they share space and, sometimes, a placenta. Most share a birthday. Infant multiples may share a crib, the milk from their mother's breasts, and most of their clothing.

Despite their parents' best efforts to endow them with ownership, multiples will most likely battle for custody over every toy and plaything that crosses their path. However, they'll generously share every germ and virus that comes their way. Of course, they'll share lots of fun, too, commemorating milestones and making happy memories together as they grow up. As playmates, they will have access to instant stimulation and constant companionship, often relieving parents of the burden of providing entertainment for their children.

While some might argue that shared DNA makes them more compatible, the consensus among parents of multiples seems to indicate that this has no bearing on their relationship. Sometimes identical twins don't get along simply because they are too similar, while fraternal multiples craft an incredibly close bond due to their shared environment.

Give and Take

Whether it is a parent's attention, the right to be first, or sole ownership of a plaything they're after, multiples can be extremely competitive with one another. Many multiples are able to channel their competitive natures into achievement when they grow older, excelling in sports or academics.

Mommy Knows Best

You might wonder, do identical twins have a closer bond than fraternal twins?

Sometimes the dynamic between a pair of multiples is one of compensating, rather than competing. Where one is lacking in a character attribute or skill, the other will step up to the plate. For example, many multiples exhibit delays in language development because the twin with stronger language skills will do most of the talking for her weaker sibling, communicating for both of them.

Different Types of Twins— Zygosity Explained

Most people are familiar with the terms *identical* and *fraternal*, but the categorizations don't represent twin type as accurately as the more scientific classifications of zygosity. Scientifically speaking, there are two basic types of multiples. Monozygotic, or identical, multiples are the result of a single zygote, or fertilized egg, while dizygotic (or multizygotic) multiples form from two or more zygotes. These multiples are commonly termed *fraternal*. All twins fit into one of these categories. Triplets, quadruplets, and other higher order multiples may be one or the other, or even a combination of both. For example, two children in a set of triplets may be monozygotic while the third is dizygotic. Twin typing, or determining zygosity, means figuring out which of these two types of multiples you have.

To understand zygosity, you have to start at the very beginning: conception. It starts when a woman's ovary releases an egg, or oocyte, into her fallopian tube and it travels toward the uterus. This process is called ovulation, and happens monthly. Along the way, sperm released by a male during sexual intercourse try to intercept the oocyte. If a sperm is able to penetrate, the egg becomes fertilized. The fertilized oocyte continues its journey to the uterus, dividing and combining cells to form a zygote. It implants in the uterus and begins to grow into a baby. But variations in the process can produce multiples—twins, triplets, or more. Zygosity not only defines twin type, but can give parents valuable insight into their multiples' origin.

What *Actually* Happens

Sometimes during the ovulation process, the ovaries are prompted to release multiple eggs. There are many reasons for this occurrence. A normal female body has two ovaries, one on the left side and one on the right. Both contain thousands of eggs. Generally the ovaries take turns ovulating, but occasionally they will each release an egg in a single cycle. Some women have a genetic tendency to hyperovulate, or release numerous eggs every month. Other women

Mommy Must

Determining the zygosity of your multiples is significant on several levels. First, it's helpful to understand how and why you became pregnant with multiples. But, more importantly, determining zygosity is important in identifying certain medical issues associated with twinning.

might release multiple eggs on an occasional basis due to hormonal fluctuations. Sometimes hormones are influenced medically, by taking drugs such as birth control pills or fertility enhancements such as Clomid or Pergonal. But they can also be impacted by a woman's age (older women tend to release multiple eggs more often than younger women), or by lifestyle (the dairy products consumed by modern women contain hormones that can effect ovulation).

Dizygotic twins are conceived if two eggs are fertilized by sperm (*di* meaning two and *zygotic* referring to the fertilized egg, or zygote). If both zygotes implant in the uterus, you've got twins! Likewise, three zygotes result in triplets and four would be quadruplets. Generally, even higher order multiples that are born of separate zygotes are all referred to as dizygotic, although a more correct term would be multizygotic.

Dizygotic Defined

Dizygotic twins are essentially siblings that happen to be born at the same time. They are each formed from a separate egg and a separate sperm. Just as related children within a family have a variety of appearances and characteristics based on the combination of genetic traits they inherit from their parents, dizygotic twins can also be very alike or very different. They can be boys, girls, or one of each.

When people talk about twins being hereditary or skipping a generation, they are referring to dizygotic twins. Women with a gene for hyperovulation are more likely to conceive twins since they routinely release multiple eggs. Their daughters have an increased chance of having twins as well, if they inherit the gene. If a woman gives birth to a son, his impact on the twinning process is irrelevant, as men do not have ovaries or ovulate. However, his daughter may inherit the hyperovulation tendency and produce twin grandchildren, thus causing the gene to "skip" a generation.

Causes of Dizygotic Twinning

Many other interesting characteristics influence dizygotic twinning. A woman's chances of conceiving dizygotic twins increase when:

- She's had a previous multiple pregnancy.
- She's over age forty-five.
- She's above average height or has a Body Mass Index above 30.
- She's already had several other children.
- She is a dizygotic twin herself, or her mother or maternal grandmother was a twin.
- She has irregular sexual intercourse.
- She conceives shortly after discontinuing birth control pills.
- She consumes dairy products.

The radical rise in the multiple birth rate since the latter part of the twentieth century is mostly observed among dizygotic multiples. It's generally attributed to the impact of advancing maternal age as women put off childbearing until they're older, which heightens their chance of releasing duplicate eggs. The increase in assisted reproduction and fertility enhancements is another contributing factor.

Monozygotic Twins

As opposed to dizygotic twins, monozygotics form from a single zygote. (*Mono* means one.) For reasons yet to be exactly determined by science, a single fertilized egg sometimes splits into two individual zygotes; both begin the process of dividing and combining cells to form embryos, resulting in two babies.

No one knows exactly what causes an egg to split. Several theories have been formulated, but none are accepted as fact. Some scientists believe that it is related to the age of the egg, while others suggest that an enzyme in certain sperm is the cause. But no one knows for sure, and monozygotic twinning remains one of the great magical mysteries of life. A zygote can split more than once. Some triplets, quadruplets, and even a documented case of quintuplets, the Dionne sisters, are monozygotic.

Mindful Mommy

Dizygotic twins generally outnumber monozygotics by about two to one. Interestingly, monozygotic twinning rates remain steady despite an overall increase in multiple birth. Further, monozygotic rates are the same across populations; you're equally likely to have identical twins whether you're Japanese or African.

Because they have formed from a single zygote, monozygotic twins share the same genetic makeup. Since many human physical characteristics are determined by genetics, monozygotic twins may share a remarkable resemblance. This is why the term "identical" is a common way to describe them. However, environmental influences also affect appearance, so no two twins are ever exactly alike.

Monozygotic twins are always of the same sex. The only exception is an extremely rare condition where a chromosomal abnormality in male monozygotic twins results in the loss of a Y chromosome in one of them, producing a female afflicted with Turner's syndrome, or "45,X."

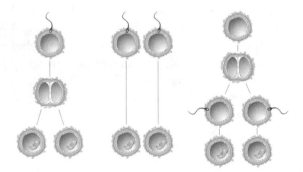

Monozygotic (identical) twins form from a single egg that splits after fertilization. Dizygotic (fraternal) multiples result when more than one egg is fertilized. Polar body twins are the result of a single ova that splits prior to fertilization.

Other Zygosity Variations

Although monozygotic and dizygotic are the two accepted categories of twinship, there are some subtypes that deserve mention. You may or may not be able to determine whether your multiples fit into one of these categories, but they are interesting to consider.

Polar Body Twins

You may have heard of a third type of twinning. Usually this refers to polar body twinning, also known as "half-identical" twins. It's more of a theory than a scientifically accepted fact, but it can provide a tidy explanation for dizygotic twins with a strong resemblance. A polar body is a small cell within the egg that divides off and usually degenerates and dies after fertilization. If, for some reason, the polar body divides off prematurely from the egg, it may also become fertilized by a sperm and develop as an embryo. No one is sure why or how it happens, and it appears to be very rare.

Developing from a single egg but separate sperm, these twins share about 75 percent of their genotypes: 50 percent from their mother, but only 25 percent

Mommy Knows Best

In 2007, researchers identified a set of twins as semi-identical. The three-year-old twins were described as sharing 100 percent of their mother's genes, but only 50 percent of their father's. They were believed to have formed when two sperm simultaneously fertilized a single egg, which then split and developed as two embryos.

from their father. They would be more "identical," or similar in appearance, than dizygotic twins but less so than monozygotics. At this time, there isn't a way to definitively determine the existence of polar body twinning; zygosity testing services that analyze DNA do not include polar body testing in their results.

Dizygotic Variances

Although polar body twinning is considered an alternate twin type, other categories are merely subsets or special types of either monozygotic or dizygotic twinning. Among dizygotic twins, two unique divergences have been identified.

Superfetation occurs when a second egg is inadvertently released in a subsequent reproductive cycle despite the fertilization of the first. The result is multiples that are conceived at different times, up to twenty-four days apart. Superfetation may account for discrepancies in fetal size and development in dizygotic multiples. If confirmed during the pregnancy, the "older" baby may be delivered days or even weeks before his twin to promote optimal gestational well-being.

Superfecundation, on the other hand, describes a situation where dizygotic twins have different fathers. It happens when an ovulating woman has intercourse with multiple partners within a short time frame. Two eggs are fertilized by sperm from different men. Several cases of superfecundation have been identified and confirmed by DNA testing, including a case in Europe in the 1970s where the babies were of different races.

Mirror Image Twins

Mirror image twins are an example of a special type of monozygotic twins. About 23 percent of monozygotic twins are classified as "mirror image," in that they exhibit reversed asymmetry in certain physical characteristics. For example, hair whorls rotate in opposite directions, moles or birthmarks are featured on opposite sides of the body, or the two have opposite hand preferences. In very rare cases, vital organs may develop on opposite sides of their bodies.

There's no way to diagnostically confirm mirror image twins, except by observation of their features. It's believed that mirror image twinning occurs due to a delayed split, about a week after fertilization, when the developing embryo has a clearly established right and left side. Mirror image twins generally share a placenta and other characteristics of monozygotic twins.

Conjoined Twins

Conjoined twins are a type of monozygotic multiples, originating from a single zygote that splits into two. However, they take their time splitting apart, with the consequence that they do not entirely separate, and begin to develop with connected tissue or organs. With an increase in media attention focused on conjoined twins, it may seem that they are becoming more common. However, conjoined twins are an extremely rare type of monozygotic twins, representing only 1 in 50,000 pregnancies.

Modern medical technology makes surgical separation of conjoined twins an increasingly viable option, even when vital organs are shared. Recent success stories like the American girls Kendra and Maliyah Herrin, Egyptian brothers Ahmed and Mohamed Ibrahim, Guatemalan sisters Maria Teresa and Mara de Jesus Quiej-Alvarez, and Filipino brothers Carl and Clarence Aguirre provide hope for a healthy future.

Determining Zygosity

So how will you know what kind of multiples you have? In the past, some multiples never knew the truth about their origin. But as modern technology provides new ways to reveal the clues, conclusive information is more accessible. In some cases, doctors can even identify zygosity before the babies ever arrive.

Mommy Must

Although some conjoined twins live into old age, most are afflicted by health complications due to strain on their shared organs. It is estimated that about 50 percent of conjoined twins are stillborn, and many more do not survive more than a few days after birth. Even with a minimal connection, it is difficult for conjoined twins to lead a normal life.

Using Ultrasound

The babies' arrangement in the womb may provide some clues about their zygosity, although the signs aren't always conclusive. First, an ultrasound examination can provide a tip-off: the sex of the babies. If they are of the opposite sex, they are obviously dizygotic. However, if the gender cannot be determined, or if all babies are of the same gender, they could be either monozygotic or dizygotic.

Placenta Analysis

Doctors can also use ultrasound to examine the placenta. Studying the placenta can be helpful in determining zygosity because the placental structure of monozygotic and dizygotic twins sometimes varies.

In any pregnancy, single or multiple, the fertilized egg travels to the uterus and implants in the uterine wall; from this point it is referred to as an embryo. The process may take several days. About a week after fertilization, the placenta begins to form along the inner wall of the uterus. Dizygotic multiples will implant individually in the uterus and develop individual placentas. Monozygotic twins, on the other hand, may follow one of several courses depending on when the zygote splits. If the split occurs early, within four days post conception, monozygotics will act much as dizygotics; they'll implant separately and, at least initially, have two distinct placentas. Early-forming monozygotics can be indistinguishable from dizygotics.

The majority of monozygotics, about 70 percent, experience the split between four and eight days post fertilization. They will share a placenta and be enclosed within a shared chorion (the outer layer of the sac that contains a fetus), but will develop individually within separate and distinct amnions (the inner membrane surrounding the sac of amniotic fluid). These twins are referred to as monochorionic monozygotics. A small percentage of monozygotic twins, less than 2 percent, split after the amnion forms on or about day eight, and develop jointly within a shared amnion. Monoamniotic multiples will also share a single placenta and chorion. Doctors can often use ultrasound technology to determine the number of placentas and the structure of the chorion and amnion by identifying the membrane separating them. The absence of a distinguishing membrane may indicate monozygotic twins.

After Birth

Sometimes you can't determine the zygosity of multiples until after they are born. After your babies are delivered, your physician may examine the

Mindful Mommy

Determining zygosity before birth is tricky since the evidence is often inconclusive. Unless doctors can definitively identify two fetuses of the same gender with a shared placenta and a shared sac, they can't be sure whether the multiples are dizygotic or monozygotic. To complicate matters, two placentas may fuse together over time, appearing as a single entity.

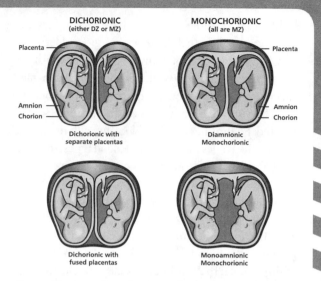

	DICHORIONIC (either DZ or MZ)	MONOCHORIONIC (all are MZ)	

Placenta

Placenta

Amnion
Chorion

Amnion
Chorion

**Dichorionic with
separate placentas**

**Diamnionic
Monochorionic**

**Dichorionic with
fused placentas**

**Monoamnionic
Monochorionic**

Depending on when the egg splits, monozygotic twins will have two separate placentas (dichorionic) that may or may not fuse together. Or they may share a single placenta (monochorionic) but have individual amniotic sacs. Monoamniotic twins are encased in a single sac.

placenta(s) visually or send them to a laboratory for pathological testing.

Most monochorionic monozygotics are identified by laboratory analysis of the placenta after birth. In the meantime, your babies may confirm or confound your suspicions by their similarities or dissimilarities. Even monozygotics may appear radically different due to their birth experience (perhaps one was a breech delivery) or factors in the uterine environment. On the other hand, some dizygotics have a strong resemblance as infants, which fades as they grow older.

What if you still don't know for sure? If you have same-sex babies that look alike but had two separate placentas, they could be either dizygotic or monozygotic. If you want to know the truth, further testing is required. Sometimes a simple blood test will reveal the secret; if the babies have different blood types, they are dizygotic. But if they share the same blood type, you'll have to take the next step and pursue a DNA test.

In most cases, doctors won't routinely order DNA testing to determine zygosity, and insurance won't cover the costs. Fortunately, several private companies now offer twin-type testing services. The process is fairly simple, the results are usually conclusive, and the cost is minimal; several companies offer the test for less than $500.

DNA testing determines zygosity by comparing cell samples from each child. Monozygotic twins, evolving from a single gene set, will have comparable samples. Dizygotic multiples, on the other hand, will exhibit differences in their DNA, since each child inherited a unique genetic package from their parents.

Mommy Knows Best

Because twins and other multiples provide scientists with such a rich resource for research, there is great interest in studying them. Many research studies will cover the cost of zygosity testing for participating multiples. It's one way to unlock the secret of your multiples' origin, while helping scientists unravel the secrets of the universe!

More and More Supertwins

The term supertwins is used to refer to multiples of three, four, or more. Another term that is commonly used is higher order multiples. More descriptive names are assigned to specifically designate the number of babies:

Three babies:	Triplets
Four babies:	Quadruplets (quads)
Five babies:	Quintuplets (quints)
Six babies:	Sextuplets
Seven babies:	Septuplets
Eight babies:	Octuplets
Nine babies:	Nonuplets
Ten babies:	Decaplets

How Higher Order Multiples Happen

Higher order multiples are conceived like anyone else, when a sperm meets an egg. Most supertwins are multizygotic, meaning that each individual embryo starts as a single egg-and-sperm combination. Sometimes a pair of individuals within the multiple set will be monozygotic and the rest will be dizygotic. In rare situations, the entire multiple set is monozygotic, the result of a fertilized egg splitting multiple times.

There's no doubt about it. If you're expecting triplets, quadruplets, or more, you've joined a rather elite club of parents. The birth rate for higher order multiples (triplets and more) jumped 380 percent between

1971 and 1995. However, despite this increase, they remain a relatively rare event.

Much of the rise in supertwin birthrates over the last thirty years is attributed to advances in reproductive technology. New techniques and procedures increase the ability to produce viable pregnancies. Elizabeth Noble, author of *Having Twins and More*, estimates that three-fourths of higher order multiples are the result of assisted conceptions.

Medical Worry: Strain on Baby and Mother

For many supertwins, merely being born seems a miraculous event. The struggle for survival in the womb puts a strain on both the mother's and babies' health. Each additional baby increases the demands on the mother's physical ability to provide sufficient space and nutrients for everyone. A supertwin pregnancy requires careful monitoring, and often, more intense medical intervention.

Multiple Challenges for the Mother

Many conditions of pregnancy are intensified in mothers of higher order multiples. Each additional baby contributes to the hormonal fluctuations raging within her body. These hormones that control pregnancy cause many of the typical symptoms such as mood swings, cravings, fatigue, and nausea; the increased levels of these hormones in a mother carrying three, four, or more babies are likely to intensify her experience of the symptoms.

Perhaps the biggest concern in higher order multiple birth is preterm labor. Because of the risk, many mothers of higher order multiples experience more medical intervention. While a twin mother may be able to avoid bed rest or hospitalization during her pregnancy, it is more common for mothers of triplets or quadruplets to require treatment to prevent preterm labor. It is virtually assured that mothers of quintuplets and higher will spend time in the hospital prior to delivery.

Every pregnancy experience is different, and not every mother of supertwins will have a complicated pregnancy. However, increased tendencies for many complications exist. For example:

- Morning sickness and nausea in early pregnancy may be intensified, leading to improper nutrition and dehydration.
- Iron-deficiency anemia is more common and severe.
- Mothers of higher order multiples are two to three times more likely to have gestational diabetes.

Mommy Knows Best

Higher order multiples are more likely to be born too early because the average uterus is designed to accommodate about ten pounds of baby. Supertwins usually weigh only half of the average birth weight of their singleton counterparts, but their combined weight easily overwhelms the capacity of the uterus. The risk increases exponentially with each additional baby.

- Complications from the placenta, such as placenta previa or abruptio placentae, are more likely to occur.
- One in three mothers of multiples will contract preeclampsia or pregnancy-induced hypertension, raising her blood pressure to dangerously unhealthy levels.
- Virtually all mothers of multiples higher than triplets will have to deliver by cesarean section, which carries an increased risk of infection, blood loss, and other complications.

If you're expecting higher order multiples, it is vital that you receive prenatal care from a physician experienced with your situation. Simply having delivered twins is not sufficient qualification for treating a woman expecting three, four, or more babies. Obstetricians and perinatologists that specialize in higher order multiples are most accessible in large cities or teaching hospitals, but they are becoming more common as the multiple birth rate increases.

In addition, you should plan to receive care from a hospital with a Level III maternity division. This designation provides assurance that the facility is prepared to meet the needs of high-risk obstetrical patients and can treat the full range of newborn afflictions once your babies are born. Some mothers choose to receive care in another city or even another state in order to ensure the best possible treatment in the event of complications.

Risks to the Babies

The biggest single risk for higher order multiples is premature birth. Without sufficient opportunity to develop in utero, premature babies are at risk for numerous complications and disabilities. Some are apparent at birth, as severely premature infants struggle to maintain the basic operation of life. Other consequences don't manifest themselves until later in life, as the children develop cognitive and motor skills.

Because prematurity is so common for the majority of higher order multiples, it's important to recognize the potential consequences and be prepared for any eventuality. It's estimated that in 40 percent of supertwin births, at least one of the babies will suffer permanent physical or neurological damage due to complications. The risk can't be underestimated.

Amid all the risks and complications, parents of higher order multiples should have optimistic hope. Advances in medical technology improve the odds for at-risk babies with every passing day. New drugs and treatments allow mothers to sustain their pregnancies longer, and neonatal care gives even extremely premature infants the opportunity to thrive.

Mindful Mommy

A normal singleton gestation is forty weeks. According to Mothers of Supertwins (MOST), the average gestational age for triplets is 33.4 weeks. For quadruplets, it is 31 weeks. And for quintuplets, it is only 28.6 weeks.

How to Prepare for Supertwins

It's not uncommon for families to have three, four, or five children. However, having them all at once is a completely different scenario! As you read through this book to prepare yourself for the birth of multiples, there are several things that you should keep in mind.

First of all, once the babies arrive, you'll be immediately outnumbered. Where parents of twins can divide their time equally between two babies, you'll always have someone waiting in the wings for your attention. In this type of situation, it is essential that you establish routines to ensure that everyone's needs are met.

Secondly, every additional baby represents an increase. Everything is "more." You'll need more help, have to buy more supplies, and require more medical monitoring. At the same time, your babies will likely have less time in your womb, so it's vital that you make the most of your pregnancy. You'll have to eat more—and gain more weight—than a mom of a singleton, or even twins. You'll need to get more rest and spend more time off your feet.

Finally, even though there are more demands, the rewards also increase exponentially. Your children will enjoy the spotlight of their special status as supertwins. They will share a unique bond with their same-age siblings. Your family will include a ready-made playgroup. And as parents, you can look forward to three times the smiles, four times the giggles, or five times as many hugs!

Chapter 2

First Things First

So you're pregnant! You may or may not even know that you're having multiples during the first twelve weeks of your pregnancy, but it is definitely a time of discovery, surprising physical changes, and emotional upheaval. If you've been pregnant before, you may think you know what to expect, but there are some unexpected differences when you're pregnant with more than one.

Is There a Way to Tell It's More than One?

Some mothers are fully aware that they are pregnant with two or more babies from the very beginning of their pregnancy. They may have strong and accurate powers of intuition or, more likely, they are under the supervision of a reproductive specialist who is monitoring every step of the conception process. However, most women who spontaneously conceive twins, triplets, or more won't begin to suspect anything out of the ordinary until their pregnancy progresses.

Suspicious Signs

Any of the following indicators may come up in the first trimester. If you experience them to an unusually extreme degree, it may be a sign that you are carrying multiples.

Weight gain: A singleton mother gains, on average, five to seven pounds in the first trimester. Anything more could indicate multiples . . . or excessive junk food consumption!

Abdomen size: With multiple babies in her womb, a pregnant woman tends to outgrow her regular clothing and require maternity gear sooner. Although it is difficult to estimate fundal size (the size of the uterus) in early pregnancy, sometimes an increase is evident, indicating multiple babies.

Fatigue: Excessive fatigue is one of the most commonly reported complaints of mothers of multiples in the early stages of pregnancy. With their bodies busy taking care of the babies, there

Mommy Knows Best

Multiples manifest their presence in several ways, but no one symptom distinguishes itself as a clear indicator. Some mothers of multiples report a strong suspicion based on one factor or combination of signals, while others experience absolutely nothing out of the ordinary.

is little energy left over for carrying out their daily routines.

Fetal movement: It's very unusual for a mother to experience fetal movement in the first trimester, yet there is some evidence to suggest that the sensation is more acute when there is more than one baby moving around.

Nausea: Extra babies can intensify the symptoms of morning sickness, such as nausea and vomiting.

You may be aware of some or all of these indications, or none at all. Perhaps your doctor or midwife brought the symptoms to your attention during a routine exam. However, they are also all normal consequences of pregnancy, which makes it quite difficult to tell whether they are truly a sign of multiples.

A Certain Something

In addition to physical symptoms, many mothers of multiples report an unexplainable hunch or vague suspicion early in pregnancy. Often it's triggered by unusual circumstances that bring multiples to the forefront of their attention. Perhaps they dream about having twins, or find themselves running across several sets of multiples in a public place. Or they may encounter mysterious phenomena that occur in sets of twos or threes. One expectant mother of twins discovered that the eggs she'd bought for holiday baking all contained double yolks; two days later an ultrasound revealed that she was having twins!

Hearing Heartbeats

You might assume that multiple babies would be easily identified by listening for multiple heartbeats. Unfortunately, that is not an effective practice in early pregnancy. Distinct heartbeat sounds are usually only detected toward the end of the first trimester, about week twelve. Even then, what sounds like an additional baby might actually be an echo of the mother's own beating heart. In other situations, multiple babies that are positioned fairly close together in the womb may have indistinguishable rhythms that are misinterpreted as a single heartbeat.

Your Body—What to Expect in the First Trimester

The first twelve weeks of a pregnancy are a very busy time, physically, for a mother of multiples. While your mind may be slow to adjust to the concept of having twins, triplets, or more, your body wastes no time in preparing to accommodate their needs in the womb. There are many different ways that you

Mindful Mommy

You can't always believe your ears. The phenomenon of a single audible heartbeat is particularly common with monochorionic monozygotics. Not only do they have similar heart rhythms, but they tend to settle close to each other because they are contained in the same sac.

will experience the effects of the marvelous miracles growing inside you. In many aspects, the early pregnancy experience for mothers of multiples is very similar to a singleton situation. Some of the symptoms may be exaggerated, but they are generally of the same nature.

Changes in Your Digestive System

The impact on your digestive system is one of the most acute—and uncomfortable—side effects of pregnancy. Fluctuating hormones decrease the muscle tone of your stomach and intestines and slow down your ability to move food through the digestive tract. At the same time, your digestive organs are being crowded by your expanding uterus. The result? Heartburn, indigestion, nausea, vomiting, constipation, or a combination of all of the above!

Although it's called "morning sickness," this unpleasant stomach distress can occur at any hour of the day or night. Just as your appetite increases, your ability to process the food decreases. Everything may smell and taste different. You may crave foods that you didn't care for previously, while your stomach turns at the mere thought of old favorites. Believe it or not, morning sickness may actually be your body's way of protecting your unborn babies.

Some researchers believe that the nausea and vomiting are a way of ridding your body of potentially toxic chemicals and protecting the fetuses from harmful food-borne bacteria.

Every woman copes with morning sickness differently. What works as a solution for one pregnant woman may make symptoms worse in another. Trial and error will help you find the best remedy for your situation. Take heart; it's a temporary condition of pregnancy, and your symptoms will likely be alleviated by the second trimester.

Here are some common recommendations for relieving morning sickness:

- Graze. Small, frequent meals and regular snacks keep your stomach happy.
- Avoid greasy or fatty foods. They take longer to digest and stay in your stomach longer.
- Stay away from spicy fare. It can aggravate symptoms by irritating your stomach tissue.
- Have someone else prepare the food. Cooking odors may trigger nausea.
- Nibble on bland snacks that are high in carbohydrates and protein, such as whole grain crackers, low-fat yogurt, or nuts.
- Wear a nausea-controlling acupressure band, such as those sold to combat seasickness.

Mindful Mommy

Morning sickness can be harmful if the vomiting becomes severe or excessive enough to result in dehydration. The condition, called hyperemesis gravidarum, occurs in about 5 percent of multiple pregnancies and requires medical treatment. Let your doctor know if you are unable to keep down any food or fluids over a twenty-four hour period.

- Talk to your doctor about homeopathic remedies such as ginger or vitamin B_6 supplements.
- Don't rush out of bed in the morning. Give yourself time to relax and your stomach will too.

Changes in Your Circulatory System

Your circulatory system will also experience major changes during pregnancy. Blood flows to and from the placenta(s) to deliver oxygenated blood and extract unoxygenated blood from the babies. There is a drastic increase in the amount of blood (blood volume) that your body has to circulate. Each additional baby increases the volume by about 10 percent.

You'll notice the impact of the increased blood volume in many different parts of your body. Swollen blood vessels in your nose and sinuses may cause stuffiness or even nosebleeds. Your gums may bleed when you brush or floss your teeth. Some women's heart rate becomes elevated.

Your breasts may become swollen and sensitive. The nipples and areolae may darken and you might

Mommy Knows Best

That extra radiance known as "pregnancy glow" isn't simply a symptom of happiness at having multiples. It's caused by an increase in blood flowing close to the skin's surface. Enjoy the glow, but also be careful. Your skin may react more sensitively to the sun or skin-care products.

notice prominent blue veins, especially if your skin is particularly fair. Many women find that their bras are one of the first things they outgrow during pregnancy. Some mothers of multiples gain two or three cup sizes by the end of their pregnancy.

The pressure of the extra blood flow causes your veins to dilate. This phenomenon is the cause of varicose veins, one of the unfortunate effects of pregnancy that doesn't disappear after delivery. Another particularly unpleasant consequence is the development of hemorrhoids, which occurs when the veins around the rectum become enlarged and protruding. Many mothers of multiples have to contend with the resulting itching and discomfort throughout their pregnancy.

Drinking lots and lots of fluids, particularly water, helps your body accommodate the production of all that extra blood. You'll also benefit by upping your iron intake. You might notice that you're craving iron-rich foods such as red meat or leafy green vegetables. It's a good idea to discuss your iron intake requirements with your doctor, who might recommend supplements.

Other Early Effects and Your Lifestyle

Some of the early effects of pregnancy are difficult to distinguish from your body's normal functions. But when there's more than one baby in the womb, these manifestations of impending maternity may be experienced more intensely. They are often a clue that there's something different about this pregnancy.

Fatigue

The one symptom most commonly experienced by expectant mothers of multiples appears to be fatigue. From occasional drowsiness to overwhelming exhaustion, nearly every pregnant woman feels her body's call to slow down and rest. It's not hard to imagine why. Before pregnancy, your body kept itself pretty busy taking care of your own needs. Now it has to attend to the demands of two, three, or even more additional beings. With the busy baby-building boom going on, there's not much energy left over for mom!

It's important to listen to your body's cues and give it the rest it requires. Take naps, go to bed earlier in the evening, and sleep late when possible. Fatigue is generally temporary, and most overwhelming during the first trimester. There is really no remedy for it, except to give in and rest.

Mommy Must

Because the first trimester is such a crucial time in your babies' development, it's important that you do your best to take care of your body. Tobacco use, alcohol, exposure to toxic substances, and even stress can contribute to defects and disabilities and should be avoided.

Spotting or Bleeding

It's normal to have some spotting or bleeding during the first trimester, but that doesn't mean that it's not frightening. The appearance of blood can make an already emotional pregnant woman frantic with worry. The most common type of bleeding during the first trimester of pregnancy is sometimes called implantation bleeding. It coincides with the timing of the first missed period and is often misinterpreted as the onset of menstruation. Instead, it is merely a result of the fertilized eggs burrowing into the soft lining of the uterus. It is usually lighter than a menstrual period and should only last a day or so.

Bleeding or spotting can also occur for a variety of other reasons in the first trimester and does not necessarily indicate an impending miscarriage. The majority of women who experience bleeding go on to have a healthy pregnancy. You should, however, notify your doctor or midwife, especially if the blood is bright red or accompanied by cramping, pain, or fever.

Your Emotional State

There is nothing quite as shocking as the surprising revelation that you are carrying multiples. Whether you find out immediately after an assisted conception, or late into your pregnancy, the discovery that you are carrying two, three, or more babies pushes your pregnancy into a new dynamic. Suddenly you are labeled a "high-risk pregnancy." Immediately there are more worries. Along with a new level of excitement, the questions loom. What will go wrong? How will we cope? Can we afford this?

Your fluctuating hormones only serve to heighten the emotion of the moment. You may find yourself hysterically laughing at your unbelievable fortune one minute, then sobbing with distress the next. Mood swings are a normal consequence of pregnancy. The surging hormones affect the neurotransmitters in your brain that control your feelings; the sensation often peaks in the last half of the first trimester.

Don't fret if you feel overwhelmed or out of control. You still have several months to prepare for your new arrivals, and you'll be able to put that time to good use. Educating yourself about multiple birth— by reading this book, for example—is an excellent way to get a handle on your situation. As you learn more, you'll feel better equipped to handle the adventures ahead.

How Your Babies Start to Develop

Your babies have been very busy since their conception. They've evolved from a sperm and an egg into a zygote, traveled down the fallopian tubes, implanted in the uterus to become an embryo, and established a placenta. At the end of the first trimester, they officially graduate from embryos to fetuses, as they will be known for the duration of the pregnancy.

Setting up shop in your womb, they've developed within a cushioning fluid-filled sac called the amnion, where they lie protected by a second membrane called the chorion. Depending on their zygosity and exactly how the development of the zygotes began, two co-multiples may be sharing the space.

As early as four weeks post-conception, the embryos have established the foundation for many of their major organs. In each embryo a tiny heart beats. A brain and a primitive central nervous system have formed. By eight weeks, the skeletal system forms a network of bones and many organ systems begin to function. At the end of the first trimester, the babies will be about the size of a travel tube of toothpaste and weigh about an ounce apiece.

The Truth About Weight Gain

Most women are particularly concerned with how their pregnancy will impact their body. Gaining weight is a given during pregnancy, and as you might expect, the amount of weight increases in a multiple pregnancy. In a singleton pregnancy, the average woman gains between twenty-five and thirty pounds. Only a third of that is fat and maternal tissue; the rest is a combination of the baby, placenta, amniotic fluid, and increased blood volume. When you double or triple the number of babies, you can expect the amount to increase proportionately.

What to Gain

The amount of weight that you gain during your multiple pregnancy is dependent on a number of factors. Your pre-pregnancy size is one determinant. If you are overweight before becoming pregnant you'll need to gain less than if you were underweight. Your doctor can advise you as to the optimal amount for your individual situation, but a general guideline is thirty-five to forty-five pounds for twins, up to fifty-five pounds for triplets, and ten additional pounds per baby for higher order multiples.

Excessive weight gain can produce its own set of problems, during pregnancy and beyond. Gestational diabetes, high blood pressure, and even postmenopausal breast cancer have been linked to unhealthy weight accumulation during pregnancy. In order to strike the right balance and achieve a healthy weight gain for both yourself and your babies, you need to be more aware of your weight fluctuations, beginning with the first trimester.

Recommended Weight Gain in Multiple Pregnancy (in pounds)

Multiples	First Trimester	Second Trimester	Third Trimester	Total
Twins	5–10	15–20	10–20	35–45
Quadruplets	10–15	25–35	20–25	50–75
Quintuplets Plus	10–20	25–35	25–30	65–100

When to Gain

By the end of the first trimester, you will likely see the scale inch upward, especially after the tenth week. Some of the increase, about two pounds, can be attributed to the extra blood volume and retained fluid. The rest is primarily accumulated body fat. Some women, depending on the severity of their morning sickness or the shape they were in pre-pregnancy, actually lose weight. Your initial prenatal visit with your doctor or midwife is an excellent opportunity to discuss the issue. At that time, your caregiver should assess your weight goals based on your individual situation.

The timetable of your weight gain is every bit as important as the amount. In a normal singleton pregnancy, weight gain is minimal in the first trimester, usually less than five pounds. However, some would say that when you're carrying multiples, an earlier weight gain produces healthier babies, based on the assumption that multiple pregnancies are often cut short due to preterm delivery, so more weight has to be gained in a shorter amount of time. Unlike a singleton pregnancy, where most weight is accumulated in the later months, weight gain may be accelerated in the earlier months with multiples.

Gaining steadily throughout the first and second trimesters helps you establish extra stores of fat and nutrients. The babies will rely on those stockpiled deposits in later pregnancy when their nutritional demands are greater.

In the second trimester, you should aim to gain one to one-and-a-half pounds per week, depending on your situation and the number of babies that you're carrying. In the first trimester, decreased appetite due to the effects of morning sickness may have inhibited your weight accumulation. Take advantage of your ravenous appetite in mid-pregnancy to feed yourself—and your babies—plenty of nutritious food.

Think Positive

For many women, weight gain carries complex psychological and emotional baggage. The idea of gaining nearly fifty pounds or more can be frightening. Try to keep it in perspective. Gaining the weight is a good thing; it's a sign of healthy development for your babies. Remember, too, that a good percentage of your weight gain will be lost at delivery. Finally, keep in mind that you're not just adding pounds; you're adding two or more new members to your family. In comparison, you'd likely accumulate more weight if you had serial singleton pregnancies.

Mommy Knows Best

The amount of weight you gain in the first half of your pregnancy has a significant impact on your babies' development in the second half. The pounds you accumulate now will help sustain them later.

Choosing a Doc with Care

Choosing a medical practitioner is one of the most important decisions that you will make during your pregnancy, affecting many aspects of your experience. You will spend many hours in this person's office in the next few months, and your choice will ultimately impact how, where, and when your babies make their entry into this world. You should examine all your options and put some thoughtful consideration into your decision.

Depending on how your pregnancy was initiated, you may already be under the care of a doctor, nurse, or midwife. If your multiples were conceived as a result of fertility enhancements, your reproductive specialist may have referred you to a caregiver. Or maybe you have already been seeing a family practitioner, doctor, or midwife during your pregnancy, but now that you know you are having more than one baby, aren't sure if you need more specialized care.

Family Practitioner

Many doctors in family practice also provide prenatal care for pregnant women and some even deliver babies. While that is fine for routine pregnancies,

Mindful Mommy

Finding out that you're expecting twins or multiples may mean a change of course for your medical care. The right doctor for your singleton pregnancy may not be the best option for your multiples. Be flexible about the change to give your babies the best possible care.

having twins or more puts you in a different class of risk, and your family doctor may not be able to provide the best care for you and your babies. You will have to weigh your options; are you more comfortable in the care of a trusted physician with whom you have a prior relationship or are you better off with a specialist who is experienced in multiple birth?

Ob-Gyn

The most common choice for pregnancy and birth care is an obstetrician-gynecologist, or ob-gyn. This type of doctor specializes in care of women. Obstetrics focuses specifically on birth and the associated issues of pregnancy, labor, delivery, and postpartum care, while gynecology is the branch of medicine dealing with diseases and routine care of the female reproductive system. The certification of ob-gyn covers both areas, but some doctors prefer to specialize only in gynecology and choose not to deliver babies.

Perinatologist

A perinatologist is even more specialized than an ob-gyn, with extra qualifications specifically in handling high-risk pregnancies. Perinatologists undergo training beyond the regular obstetrics residency, spending three additional clinical years in research and patient care. They are the top professionals for diagnosing and treating medical conditions that threaten the health of the mother or babies during pregnancy. Because they deal with high-risk situations, perinatologists often have a richer depth of experience with multiple birth. In addition, they are usually associated with leading hospital facilities and have access to the latest and greatest technology for diagnosing and treating the conditions that might affect your babies' health.

Midwives and Doulas

Many women are returning to the use of midwives for care during pregnancy and childbirth. A certified nurse-midwife (CNM) is licensed to practice after obtaining a degree in nursing and completing specialized training as a midwife. These women generally provide a more individualized approach to care, focusing on the patient's goals for her childbirth experience.

Midwives are not usually equipped to handle high-risk pregnancies and deliveries. Because of the risks associated with multiples, expectant mothers are often discouraged from considering a midwife. However, the advantages of utilizing the services of a midwife are underestimated. Many CNMs are fully capable of handling the needs of uncomplicated twin deliveries, and occasionally even higher order multiples.

Mindful Mommy

Any midwife who truly values her patient's well-being will work in conjunction with an obstetrician or perinatologist. If you are considering a midwife's services during your pregnancy with multiples, ensure that she can readily provide access to other health-care professionals if you encounter any complications.

If your heart is set on a midwife but your body just won't cooperate, a doula may be a good compromise. A doula is a professional birth assistant who acts as your advocate in a medical setting. She is trained in the physiology of birth and is also equipped to help you cope with the emotional aspects of childbirth. She will provide support, physical comforting, and an objective perspective about the events surrounding the birth of your multiples. Studies have shown that women who use the services of a doula have faster labors, decreased use of epidurals, and fewer c-sections.

You can hire a doula to attend you during labor, delivery, and even after the babies are born. Many doulas are trained as lactation consultants and can assist with breastfeeding. They can also provide an extra set of hands when caring for your new infants. They may even be available prior to delivery, offering their services as a caregiver if you are on bed rest.

Mindful Mommy

Doulas aren't cheap. They can charge from a few hundred to over a thousand dollars, depending on how long you utilize their services. Despite the benefits, few insurance companies will cover the cost. The extra support may be well worth the expense, however, especially for parents of multiples.

Chapter 3

The Long
(and Sometimes Bumpy)
Road

As you grow accustomed to the idea of having multiples—and grow physically!—you are likely to experience a period of relief and rejuvenation in the middle phase of pregnancy, as the nausea and exhaustion gives way to a period of enhanced energy and vitality. Then, the third trimester may feel like an eternity to a pregnant mother who is growing increasingly eager to meet her babies, yet anxious that they don't show up too early.

Your Changing Body in the Second Trimester

The second trimester brings good news and bad news. Some of the problems that plagued you during the early weeks of pregnancy will start to dissipate, such as the nausea and queasiness of morning sickness and the extreme exhaustion. However, in their place, some new symptoms may make an appearance. By this time it is generally very difficult to conceal your pregnancy. The height of your fundus, the name for the top of your uterus, exceeds that of a singleton pregnancy by several inches. In fact, by the end of the second trimester, you may have the appearance of a full-term singleton pregnancy, causing you to attract concern for your "imminent" delivery.

What You're Feeling

Your appetite may increase to ravenous proportions. Take advantage of your hunger to fill up on healthy foods, such as lean proteins, fresh fruit and vegetables, and whole grains. As your constant urge to urinate eases, you may find it easier to sleep through the night. However, you may be visited by frequent, vivid dreams.

One physical phenomenon that pregnant mothers of multiples are particularly prone to is round ligament pain, sharp pinching discomfort in the abdominal area. It occurs as the ligaments that support your uterus stretch to accommodate its rapid expansion. Sometimes it will happen when you move or stretch suddenly, or it can come out of the blue, even while you're at rest. Aside from the discomfort, it can be an alarming experience if you confuse the sensation with the onset of contractions. Round ligament pain usually eases after a moment, but if it recurs, be sure to discuss your symptoms with your doctor.

As you grow, your skin stretches to cover your expanding abdomen. Stretch marks may make an appearance on your breasts, belly, or hips. They indicate a separation of collagen, a substance that lends elasticity to skin. They may be pink or purplish, but will probably fade to a light silvery shadow after pregnancy. Stretch marks don't hurt, but they may feel tight or itchy. Lotions or oils can decrease the discomfort.

Some other common symptoms that you may experience during these middle months are

- Constipation
- Swelling (edema)
- Nasal stuffiness
- Bleeding gums
- Headaches

There is some good news. Many women attain a radiant appearance during this period of pregnancy. The extra circulation drives more blood to the hair follicles, skin surface, and nail beds. The result? Thick, lustrous hair; clear, luminous skin; and strong nails that grow faster than you can say "manicure." Enjoy the beauty effects of this special time!

Changes in Sexual Desire

After a few months of wanting sleep rather than sex, you may experience an awakening in the second trimester. Many moms, and appreciative dads, report an increase in sexual desire during this time. Sometimes extreme concern about preterm labor may prompt your caregiver to recommend abstinence, but unless you've been advised to restrict sexual activity, you can take advantage of your increased appetite. Most couples will enjoy a second honeymoon period before the advancing pregnancy literally gets in the way of sexual relations.

Maternity Clothes: Dressing for Success

It's time to go shopping! By the second trimester, you'll have outgrown your pre-pregnancy outfits and will require maternity clothing. Before you spend a bundle on new attire, you'll want to consider the big picture, which is growing bigger every week! While you should have no problem fitting into standard maternity styles during the middle trimester, you may need to update your wardrobe every few weeks to accommodate your escalating girth.

The most important factor in choosing clothing is comfort. Choose soft, flexible fabrics with a bit of stretch. Recent fashion trends have produced new styles of maternity clothing that sit below the belly, instead of stretching across it, and many women find this a more comfortable option. It's also more practical for moms of multiples, whose bellies exceed the measurements of the average pregnancy.

By the third trimester, you may find that you've outgrown your maternity wardrobe. Aside from a tent, your options for clothing are limited. Even the largest sizes of maternity wear may not cover your expanded midsection. Many mothers find that the best option for late pregnancy is to skip the maternity store and invest in a couple of plus-size outfits. Designed to accommodate larger women, they should fit comfortably over your belly. You don't need much to carry you through these last few months; a few T-shirts and elastic-waist pants will do. You may have to sacrifice fashion for a while, but you can look forward to returning to style once the babies are born.

If you are plagued by backache and muscle discomfort, invest in an undergarment that supports the weight of your expanding belly. It helps take the pressure off of your back and can provide a great deal of relief. You'll find such products available at maternity and baby stores, and the cost may be covered by your insurance plan. Buy a product intended for late pregnancy, even if you plan to start wearing it before the third trimester. As a mother of multiples, you'll need the extra support earlier in your pregnancy.

A good bra will also provide comfort. As your breasts prepare for nursing, they are likely changing shape and size, and your pre-pregnancy bras won't fit the bill, so to speak. If you haven't already, invest in several good-quality maternity bras. If you're

Mindful Mommy

Even if you lose weight after you deliver, your feet may not ever return to their old shoe size. A pregnancy hormone called relaxin softens up joints and ligaments, including those in feet. Sometimes this causes feet to spread out and widen, and they don't always return to their pre-pregnancy shape.

planning to breastfeed, you can even consider starting to wear nursing bras. They'll do double duty, providing extra support for the last few months of your pregnancy, and easy access to your breasts once the babies arrive.

Maternity clothing can be a big expense in pregnancy. If you have any opportunity to borrow outfits, take advantage of that! Some local clubs for parents of twins organize maternity clothing swaps or sales. Consignment shops are another good option for bargains.

Staying Comfortable Toward the End

There's no doubt about it, the last few months of a multiple pregnancy can get uncomfortable. For one thing, you've expanded to accommodate two or more growing babies! You may feel gigantic, and realize that you're only growing larger. Despite your overall lack of energy and a stern admonition from your doctor to rest as much as possible, your increased girth may make it impossible to relax comfortably. Meanwhile, as they grow, the babies are putting increasing pressure on your muscles, ribs, lungs, stomach, and bladder. As the time to deliver draws near, your emotional discomfort may increase as well. Fears about your babies' safe entry into this world and your future as a family may seem more relevant as the time of their arrival gets closer.

Life in the third trimester doesn't have to be miserable, however. Keep your situation in perspective; it's temporary, after all. Despite the physical discomfort they cause inside of you, your babies are much better off in your womb than born prematurely. This is a time for frequent positive reinforcement and support; remind yourself that things could be much worse and adopt an attitude of gratitude for each extra day of nurturing that you can give your babies.

When Is It Time to Take It Easy?

If she hasn't already, your doctor may advise you to stop working during the last portion of your pregnancy. Any job that requires a lot of standing, strenuous physical activity, or long hours is probably not a good way to spend the last weeks before the babies are born. However, some mothers are able to continue at their jobs until shortly before they deliver. Discuss the risks and benefits with your medical provider if you are having twins and your job allows you to be relatively sedate and comfortable while you work. Mothers of higher order multiples will likely have less opportunity to stay on the job.

On the Go

As it gets closer to the time when your babies will arrive, your list of "to-do's" gets longer and longer. Unfortunately, you may find that you're less productive in the last trimester. You may experience difficulty getting in and out of a car; you may even need to restrict your driving if your shape prevents you from sitting safely behind the wheel. This is a great time to take advantage of Internet services and do your shopping from the comfort of home.

As relaxing as it may sound, this is not the time to plan a vacation getaway. While mothers of singletons are considered safe for air travel up to week thirty-six, that's not the case with mothers of multiples, who are at increased risk for preterm labor. Many airlines have policies denying travel to women in the last month of their pregnancy; with twins or more, you'll look like you're near your due date even if you're months away. If your doctor does give you permission to travel by air (which is unlikely in the third trimester), you will need a letter indicating that you can safely fly in order to board the aircraft.

At Home

You may feel inclined to "nest" as your due date gets closer, making your home clean and ready for the babies. Leave the heavy-duty work to someone else,

Mommy Must

If your doctor approves, use that nesting energy to make and freeze casseroles to eat later; you'll likely have less time to prepare meals when you're busy feeding the babies.

however. Activities that require heavy lifting, pushing, or climbing are simply too risky. Slaving over a hot stove isn't recommended either, although short bouts of standing in the kitchen may be acceptable.

Bed Rest

One of the greatest ironies of multiple birth is that you spend most of your pregnancy trying to avoid bed rest, but once the babies arrive, you crave it! Some form of bed rest is a reality for many mothers of multiples during their pregnancy, as a means of preventing preterm labor or diminishing the effects of problems that would otherwise result in the loss of one or all of the babies.

Your condition will determine whether partial or complete bed rest will be most beneficial to your babies. Often the first stage is decreased or reduced activity, sometimes a routine recommendation in the final weeks of pregnancy. A next step is partial bed rest, also called modified or moderate bed rest. You may be advised to spend a certain number of hours in bed each day or, conversely, you may be allotted a specified amount of time out of bed.

Mindful Mommy

Because partial or modified bed rest leaves you with a lot of freedom to control your activity, it's important that you not overdo it. Ask your doctor for explicit instructions as to what is allowed or discouraged.

Complete bed rest is stricter, requiring you to remain in bed twenty-four hours a day, with bathroom breaks. In extreme situations you may find yourself confined to bed in the hospital. Being admitted to the hospital during your pregnancy can be terrifying. It may feel like a prison sentence. But it can also be reassuring. You can turn over responsibility for your babies' health to professionals, and it's comforting to know that you are in the best possible place if anything goes wrong.

Waiting Patiently

As you reach the third trimester, the birth of your babies may seem imminent. With so much attention focused on the risks of preterm labor, you may be anticipating an early arrival. Even though you've made it past the critical point for survival, your babies will benefit by spending the majority of the third trimester in your womb, rather than in the hospital.

For many mothers of multiples, the last trimester is cut short. About half of twins, and the majority of higher order multiples, are born at least a month early. It's important to remain aware of the signs of preterm labor. You'll be scheduled for more frequent visits with your health-care provider so that he can assess any signs of impending labor, as well as the condition of your babies.

Preterm Labor—
What to Look Out for

Preterm labor, or the onset of cervical dilation before a baby is considered full term, is a major source of concern because it can lead to premature delivery. The fact that preterm labor is more prevalent in multiple pregnancy makes it a focus of concern for any expectant mother of twins or more. A normal singleton gestation usually lasts forty weeks, but opinions vary on the optimal gestation for multiples. Some define full term as thirty-eight weeks for twins, and thirty-six weeks for higher order multiples. (There is even some evidence to indicate that carrying babies past thirty-eight weeks in a multiple pregnancy can pose risks to the mother's health.)

The dangers can't be denied. Preterm labor can lead to premature birth. Despite amazing advances in medical technology, babies born too early simply can't survive outside the womb. The simple fact is that preterm birth is the leading cause of neonatal death, and preemies who do survive may face a lifetime of medical problems.

Mommy Knows Best

Mothers of twins are two and one-half times more likely to experience preterm labor than a singleton mother. However, preterm labor doesn't always result in disaster. Learning about the reality of preterm labor and premature birth should be a lesson in preparation and prevention, not a source of alarm and worry.

Medical providers focus heavily on raising awareness about preterm labor because, if caught in time, it can be stopped or delayed. Heightened awareness about the risks may prompt a mother to take action and get medical attention sooner rather than later. While it's not always possible to halt preterm labor, in some cases quick medical reaction can increase the chances of success.

Signs of Preterm Labor

Sometimes preterm labor is silent. Many women don't realize that their body is undermining their pregnancy until it's too late—or rather, too early for their premature babies. You won't feel an incompetent cervix dilating or effacing. You may not even feel contractions, especially if you've never been pregnant before.

The uterus contracts throughout pregnancy. These irregular, "practice" contractions are called Braxton-Hicks and they can start as early as the second trimester. As the body readies for labor and delivery, however, the timing, regularity, and intensity of the contractions will increase.

Mindful Mommy

Fetal fibronectin testing allows doctors to predict whether preterm labor is imminent, although it doesn't provide any guarantees unless the test provides a negative return. Fetal fibronectin (FFN) is a protein found in the membranes and fluid of the amniotic sac whose presence could indicate the onset of preterm labor, even when other symptoms aren't apparent.

Women experience contractions in different ways; they may produce a sensation of pain, hardening, pressure, heaviness, tightening, or cramping. They may be felt in the abdomen, pelvis, or lower back and thighs. The following symptoms and situations should be reported to your doctor or midwife:

- More than four or five contractions per hour
- Rhythmic or persistent pelvic pressure
- Cramps, similar to menstrual cramping
- Backache

While contractions are the main indicator of preterm labor, you can't count on them to let you know what's going on. There are some other signs that indicate that labor is already in progress. Should you experience the following, notify your doctor.

- Diarrhea
- Vaginal bleeding or discharge
- Uneasy sense that something is wrong

Mindful Mommy

It's the pattern and frequency of the contractions that can signal that labor is imminent. Occasional or irregular contractions are normal. Recurring contractions at a rate of more than four per hour are cause for concern and require further monitoring.

Treatment Options for Preterm Labor

If you are diagnosed with preterm labor, there are several options for treatment. Your doctor will first do an assessment of your condition. Your contractions will be monitored. Your cervix may be examined, and an ultrasound may be performed to update the status of the babies' development. Ultimately, the goal of any treatment is to prevent or delay birth until the babies are developmentally ready, whether a matter of days, weeks, or months.

Often the first attempt to stop the progress of preterm labor is to assign the mother to rest. You may be encouraged to decrease your level of activity, or may need to begin some level of bed rest. Contractions will be monitored to see if they respond to the change in activity level. You may be given a monitor to use at home, or may be asked to report to the hospital or doctor's office for occasional monitoring. If dehydration is considered a factor, oral or intravenous fluid delivery may be required.

Drugs can be used to counteract preterm labor and delay delivery. These medications, called tocolytics, act to relax the muscle of the uterus to stop it from contracting, or to counteract the hormones that

Mommy Must

Most drugs have side effects and risks. Taking them is not generally a comfortable experience for the mother. Tocolytics can raise your heart rate, making you feel shaky and jittery. Headaches, dizziness, drowsiness, nausea, and muscle cramps may also result.

are initiating the onset of labor. Usually they are first administered intravenously, but are also available in the form of a pill or injection. Ongoing treatment may require the insertion of a subcutaneous pump to deliver small doses of the medicine at regular intervals. There is a great deal of controversy associated with the use of these drugs; be sure you fully discuss the risks and benefits of their use with your doctor, and consider alternatives.

Magnesium sulfate is also commonly administered in the treatment of preterm labor. It's also used to treat preeclampsia and PIH (pregnancy-induced hypertension). It relaxes the muscles of the uterus. You will most likely be hospitalized for a few days while you receive this treatment so that you can be closely monitored for side effects. Magnesium sulfate can cause nausea, headache, weakness, and heart palpitations. Many women who take it experience a sensation of flushing and their skin feels hot.

Often, it is more effective to administer medication for the babies rather than the mother. Instead of slowing down labor, these drugs speed up the babies' development, increasing their viability at birth. In the last ten years, the use of corticosteroid therapy has greatly improved the odds for premature infants when administered twenty-four to forty-eight hours before birth. Steroids such as betamethasone or dexamethasone are injected into the mother to speed up the development of the babies' lungs and intestines to give them a better chance of survival after delivery.

Overdue and Over It

Despite the focus on preventing preterm labor, not all multiples are born early. Half of twin pregnancies last longer than thirty-six weeks. You may find yourself in the final weeks of the third trimester feeling like there is no end in sight. It can be an uncomfortable time, full of relief that your babies are close to term, but with anxiety looming about labor and delivery.

There is medical evidence to suggest that postmature pregnancy poses risks for both the babies and their mother. The discomfort of late-term pregnancy and the strain on the mother's organs may prompt doctors to intervene if labor is not imminent. Some argue that thirty-eight weeks should be considered full term for twins and recommend delivery when a mother reaches that point. Other experts maintain that forty weeks is the standard milestone, whether there is one baby or more.

Whether early or late, it's difficult to predict the exact date of your babies' arrival. Throughout the final trimester, your medical care providers will review the babies' status and your own health. Your

Mindful Mommy

Because the risk of preterm birth is heightened for multiples, much attention is focused on delivering early, rather than late. However, a review of the National Organization of Mothers of Twins Clubs' database indicates that 13 percent of its membership didn't deliver before their due date.

body may go into labor on its own—ideally, close to term, but possibly earlier. Or your doctor may recommend an intervention to deliver the babies in an effort to optimize their health or your own well-being. There are a couple of different ways to prompt labor, and the approach will depend on the reasons motivating the induction and on your physical condition. Induction serves to ripen the cervix and stimulate contractions.

There are also some natural methods of prompting labor. You should discuss these options with your medical caregiver before attempting them, but they may be worth considering before attempting a medical induction. Stimulating your nipples or having sexual intercourse to the point of orgasm may sufficiently raise your own hormones and prompt contractions. A less pleasant tradition is to swallow castor oil, a potent laxative, to activate your bowels.

Complications and Concerns

Sometimes things go wrong. There are a number of complications associated specifically with multiple birth, as well as an increased risk of other disorders that impact pregnancy. Fortunately, if diagnosed in time, many of these conditions can be remedied before the babies are even born, or shortly after birth. Let's take a look at the most common complications.

Twin-to-Twin Transfusion Syndrome

Twin-to-twin transfusion syndrome (TTTS) may sound like a plot from a science fiction movie, but it's an actual phenomenon that can occur during a monozygotic twin pregnancy. Undetected or untreated, it can have devastating consequences for the babies. However, new treatment options give doctors the ability to correct the situation and offer new hope to parents impacted by the disease.

What Is It?

TTTS, also known as feto-fetal transfusion syndrome or stuck twin syndrome, is a disease of the placenta. It doesn't make the mother sick, and its effect on the babies is environmental, not direct. In other words, the babies will begin to develop perfectly normally, but because the placenta they depend on to supply oxygen and nutrition malfunctions, they risk heart failure, brain trauma, and damage to their organs.

The placenta circulates blood and nutrients from the mother to her babies. Within a shared placenta, blood vessels can malfunction, causing an unequal exchange of blood flow between the babies. Essentially,

Mommy Knows Best

The effects of TTTS can produce a great deal of variability in the appearance of monozygotic or "identical" twins. The donor twin is usually much smaller and paler, while the recipient twin is larger with a ruddier complexion.

one fetus becomes a donor, pumping blood into the second, recipient fetus. This situation causes problems for both babies, with the donor twin not getting enough blood and the recipient receiving an excess.

The donor twin is at risk for anemia, intrauterine growth retardation, and restricted amniotic fluid (oligohydramnios). While the donor's growth is stunted, the recipient twin grows larger and larger. The extra blood overloads his circulatory system and puts him at risk for heart failure. As he struggles to process the extra blood, his urine production results in an excess of amniotic fluid (polyhydramnios). Eventually, polyhydramnios can trigger the onset of preterm labor and both babies are at risk of being born too early to survive outside the womb.

The timing of the disease ultimately determines the prognosis for the babies. It is easier to overcome later in pregnancy, when the simplest solution is to deliver the babies. Although they may face the consequences of a premature birth, they will escape the threat to their survival that exists if they remain in the womb. However, if the onset of TTTS occurs earlier, before the babies are viable, the situation is more dire.

Mindful Mommy

As the amount of fluid surrounding the recipient twin increases, the donor twin may be pushed to one side of the uterus. As her fluid levels decrease, she may appear to be stuck to the wall of the womb. Thus, the term "stuck twin syndrome" has been used to describe this condition.

There are five stages of TTTS:

Stage I: Small amount of fluid in donor baby, large amount in the recipient

Stage II: Symptoms of Stage I, along with undetectable bladder in the donor twin

Stage III: One or both babies will have evidence of poor blood flow

Stage IV: Characterized by hydrops in either baby (a fluid accumulation that signifies heart failure)

Stage V: One or both babies have succumbed

When TTTS is detected in the second trimester, it is usually termed chronic or severe. After twenty-four weeks, it is defined as moderate. When it occurs later in the third trimester, it is labeled mild or acute.

Treatment for TTTS depends on how far along you are in your pregnancy, and to which stage the disease has progressed. Fetoscopic laser surgery is available in half a dozen facilities in the United States as well as other locations in Australia and Europe. As studies confirm its success in treating TTTS, it will become more widely available in the next few years.

Mindful Mommy

TTTS only affects monozygotic twins. It occurs in about a third of monochorionic pregnancies, or less than 10 percent of all identical twins. If untreated, it has as much as an 80 percent fetal mortality rate.

The resources listed in Appendix A include contact information for TTTS support and treatment.

Mo-Mo Twins

While TTTS is inflicted upon monochorionic twins, another class of monozygotic twins is subjected to even more dangers. Monochorionic/mono-amniotic ("mo-mo") twins share not only a placenta but an amniotic sac as well. Cord entanglement is the primary risk associated with mo-mo twins as they float together in a single encasement of fluid. If the intertwining results in compression of either cord, a baby's supply of blood and nutrients from the placenta can be cut off.

Ultimately, the cure for this condition is to deliver the babies. Parents of mo-mo twins will play a waiting game throughout pregnancy, constantly monitoring the situation until the babies are viable and can be delivered.

High Blood Pressure (Hypertension)

While many complications in multiple pregnancy put the babies at risk, one in particular jeopardizes the mother. Mothers of multiples are particularly

Mindful Mommy

The survival rate for mo-mo babies is estimated at about 60 percent. However, the odds are improving as doctors experiment with new treatments to sustain the pregnancy, including a drug that reduces the amount of amniotic fluid, restricting the babies' movement and minimizing chances of entanglement.

susceptible to a group of diseases associated with elevated blood pressure.

Pregnancy-Induced Hypertension (PIH)

Increased blood pressure—generally measured as higher than 140 over 90—is common in mothers of multiples. It is treated by reducing activity, bed rest, and sometimes with medication. Generally, hypertension associated with pregnancy will dissipate as soon as the babies are born, but these women may be at risk for high blood pressure later in life, especially in subsequent pregnancies.

Preeclampsia/Toxemia

A more serious condition affecting mothers of multiples is preeclampsia, also known as toxemia. Less than 10 percent of singleton pregnancies are impacted by preeclampsia, but about one in three women expecting twins, triplets, or more will suffer from it during pregnancy. While it is often confused with hypertension, two other symptoms must be present in order for a diagnosis of preeclampsia to be confirmed: edema and elevated protein in the urine. Preeclampsia can precede a more serious condition,

Mommy Must

There is evidence to suggest that a diet rich in calcium and omega-3 fatty acids in the form of fish oil can reduce the incidence of preeclampsia in pregnancy. You should discuss the possible benefits of this with your health-care provider before taking any dietary supplements.

eclampsia, which can lead to seizures, stroke, kidney failure, a ruptured liver, and problems with blood clotting.

Preeclampsia usually affects women in the latter half of pregnancy, but the longer a woman combats it, the greater the potential for complications. There is no cure for the condition; the only remedy is to deliver the babies. Medical caregivers have to weigh the deterioration of the mother's state against the babies' outlook for survival if born early.

Notify your doctor immediately if you experience the symptoms of preeclampsia, including sudden swelling in the hands or face, rapid weight gain, blurred vision, seeing spots, intense headache, or abdominal pain. Generally, at the first sign of symptoms, you'll be advised to restrict your activity and may even be assigned to bed rest. Sometimes medications may be administered, such as magnesium sulfate, a drug commonly used to treat preterm labor that also temporarily lowers blood pressure.

HELLP Syndrome

Fifteen percent of women with preeclampsia will develop HELLP syndrome, an abbreviation for hemolysis, elevated liver enzymes, and low platelets. This condition is due to disturbance of the liver's normal function, and mothers with HELLP can die from a ruptured liver if they are not treated. Sometimes the syndrome progresses before the symptoms of preeclampsia are identified, because women can develop HELLP in the absence of hypertension, edema, and protein in the urine. Be sure to report any unusual symptoms to your doctor, such as abdominal pain on the right side, fatigue, nausea, vomiting, or headache. These can be signs of HELLP syndrome.

Gestational Diabetes

Gestational diabetes in pregnancy is not the same as a diagnosis of diabetes outside of pregnancy. Although the disorder is similar—the inability of the body to process glucose (sugar) in the blood— the cause is directly related to pregnancy, and the condition should disappear after delivery. However, it is important to get treatment, because when glucose backs up in the bloodstream, it can damage the mother's organs, and possibly the babies as well.

If you are diagnosed with gestational diabetes during your pregnancy with multiples, you will need to alter your diet. In some cases, gestational diabetes may be controlled with lifestyle and nutrition management, but if your case does not respond, you may require injections of insulin for the duration of your pregnancy. Fortunately, gestational diabetes has little effect on the babies, although they may be at risk of contracting diabetes later in life.

Mindful Mommy

Gestational diabetes occurs two to three times more often in multiple pregnancy than in singleton pregnancies. The increase is likely due to the additional hormones produced when there are extra babies; hormones can interfere with the body's ability to process the insulin produced by the pancreas.

Problems with the Placenta

The placenta plays a vital role in pregnancy, delivering nutrients and oxygen to the babies and removing their waste. In a multiple pregnancy, each baby may have his own placenta, or two babies may share a single placenta. Either way, if something goes wrong, the babies' survival is at stake.

Placenta Previa

When the placenta implants low in the uterus, covering the cervical opening, it's called placenta previa. The chances of this happening are increased when a uterus has to accommodate two or more placentas. While placenta previa does not pose a risk to the babies' development, it may cause vaginal bleeding toward the conclusion of the pregnancy, as the cervix begins to dilate and open. Bed rest may help the bleeding subside by decreasing the amount of pressure on the placenta. In extreme cases, the mother may require a blood transfusion to prevent excess blood loss. Usually she will have to deliver the babies via cesarean section.

Abruptio Placentae

Sometimes the placenta begins to detach prematurely from the wall of the uterus, a condition called abruptio placentae. While it can be caused by trauma to the abdominal region, it can also be instigated by other conditions common in a multiple pregnancy, such as high blood pressure. The detachment may be mild and partial, happening slowly over time, or complete and sudden. Pain and bleeding usually accompany complete abruption; this requires immediate delivery of the babies by c-section. In more mild cases, doctors will closely monitor the pregnancy to determine the best option for the babies, weighing the consequences of early delivery. Bed rest may be recommended.

Hemorrhage

Mothers of multiples have an increased risk of hemorrhage, or uncontrolled bleeding, during their pregnancy or following delivery. Several factors contribute to the risk:

- A uterus that is stretched and strained by accommodating additional babies
- A greater portion of the surface area of the uterus covered by placental tissue
- Increased chance of undergoing cesarean section

Usually, the only consequence is heavier postpartum bleeding following delivery, but occasion-

Mommy Knows Best

Placental abruptions are three times more common in a multiple pregnancy due to the increased stretching of the uterus as it expands to accommodate the extra babies.

ally severe, uncontrolled bleeding puts the mother's health at risk.

Intrauterine Growth Restriction (IUGR)

Multiples are particularly at risk for intrauterine growth restriction (IUGR), also known as intrauterine growth retardation. Essentially, this very wordy terminology is used to describe a small baby, a baby that is not growing at a "normal" rate according to standardized charts. Babies with IUGR are identified when they are below the tenth percentile on growth charts. IUGR occurs in more than a quarter of twin pregnancies, much more often than in the general population of singleton births, where the occurrence is only 6 percent.

What Causes It?

IUGR can occur as a result of other conditions particular to a multiple birth, such as TTTS, pre-eclampsia, or a shared placenta. But sometimes just the fact that there is more than one baby competing for resources in the womb causes the restriction in growth. IUGR is the second leading cause of death in infants.

Let's take a look at the differences between IUGR, SGA, and LBW.

IUGR refers to a baby who has not reached his growth potential because of some medical problem. An SGA (small for gestational age) baby is simply a small baby, growing to his full potential. LBW (low birth weight) is the term used to describe babies after birth, while IUGR and SGA refer to babies while they're still in the womb.

What Can Be Done?

IUGR puts babies at risk for stillbirth and neo-natal death. Often, the only option for treatment is to deliver the affected baby, or babies. They will be impacted by the usual complications associated with preterm birth, but can be treated for them. The effects of IUGR can follow the babies, even after birth. They're at risk for many long-term neurologi-cal and behavioral handicaps that may not surface until many years later. They are often hypoglycemic, and have weak muscle tone and poor circulation. Thirty percent of babies who succumb to SIDS (sud-den infant death syndrome) had IUGR.

You can take some steps to prevent IUGR from impacting your babies. Maternal nutrition is crucial. Eating healthy foods, and plenty of them, provides the energy that your babies need to grow adequately. Maternal tobacco use is a leading cause of IUGR, so it goes without saying that you should stay away from cigarettes. Finally, getting plenty of rest can also help. When you rest, nutrients will pass more easily to the babies, who utilize every calorie to grow and develop. While you can't absolutely prevent IUGR in a mul-tiple pregnancy, there is no doubt that taking tiptop care of yourself is the best way to protect your babies.

Chapter 4

Happy and Healthy Pregnancy

THERE ARE MANY STEPS you can take to preserve and even improve your overall health while you're pregnant with multiples. You know you should be eating right and getting enough sleep, but do you know exactly what that means? It's also important to be aware of the things you should avoid during pregnancy. Working along with your doctors and caregivers, you'll give your babies the best possible start in life.

Important Prenatal Tests and Assessments

Having multiples puts extra demands on the mother's body. In order to ensure the vitality of both mom and babies, it's important to make health a priority. You and your babies will go through several tests and assessments. Some are prompted by the extra risks inherent in a multiple pregnancy, while others are routine assessments that are recommended for all pregnancies.

Ultrasound

Ultrasound assessments can be a very enjoyable and reassuring test for expectant parents, offering them a peek at their developing babies. In fact, it is often the method by which a multiple pregnancy is confirmed, and perhaps your own twins, triplets, or more were revealed in the shadowy blobs of an ultrasound image. There are no known risks associated with ultrasound technology and it generates little discomfort for the mother, other than requiring her to lie flat during the procedure. You may have one ultrasound in the second trimester, but you are more likely to have several throughout a multiple pregnancy, as it is a simple, inexpensive, and relatively noninvasive diagnostic tool.

Your ultrasound may be performed by a trained sonographer, or by your obstetrician or perinatologist. Sometimes a Level II ultrasound is recommended for multiple pregnancies. This is simply a more detailed assessment. The same equipment is utilized but it is generally performed by a maternal-fetal specialist at a hospital rather than in your doctor's or midwife's office. It will likely take an hour or two, where a regular ultrasound lasts about thirty minutes.

Either way, the procedure provides much useful information. It helps to ascertain that the babies are developing on schedule, confirms their due date, and rules out potential problems. Often other details are revealed, such as the babies' genders (if you want to make them known) and perhaps even their zygosity. During the procedure, your doctor will likely spend some time trying to identify and assess the membrane that separates the babies' sac. A discernible membrane may indicate that the babies are dichorionic, although it doesn't necessarily confirm that they are dizygotic. Even monozygotic (identical) twins can be dichorionic. A thin membrane might identify monochorionic twins while the lack of a membrane might be a clue that the babies are monoamniotic. (See Chapter 1 for more on zygosity.)

Fetal Assessment

During the last trimester, you're likely to have ample opportunity to keep tabs on your babies. Fetal surveillance during the last trimester is accomplished with ultrasound and heart rate monitoring, with a variety of tests that determine the babies' condition. A non-stress test is a painless way for you to participate in assessing the babies. It's performed by your doctor, usually at about thirty weeks, although it can

Mommy Must

Determining whether your babies are boys, girls, or one of each can help establish their zygosity. Only dizygotic (fraternal) multiples can be different sexes. Identifying that there are both male and female babies rules out monozygotic multiples and the associated complications, such as twin-to-twin transfusion syndrome and monoamniotic twin issues.

be used earlier in pregnancy to monitor the impact of contractions. Testing is done with transducers that measure each baby's heart rate, and an additional monitor to record any uterine contractions. You'll be asked to sit quietly or lie down and relax. Remember, it's called a *non*-stress test, so don't be anxious! As the transducers monitor the babies' heart rates, you'll be asked to indicate your experience of fetal movement.

A non-stress test is one component of a biophysical profile, a test that gives an overall assessment of the babies' condition. It's usually recommended midway through the last trimester, beginning at about week thirty-two. It includes evaluations of each baby's heart rate activity, respiration, body movements, muscle tone, and amniotic fluid volume. It may also include an assessment of the placenta. The non-stress test provides information about the fetuses' heart rate activity, while the rest of the elements are measured via ultrasound. If one or more of the babies scores low on a biophysical profile, it may be cause for concern and may prompt consideration of an early delivery.

Alpha-fetoprotein (AFP) Test

The Alpha-fetoprotein test is also commonly referred to as a triple screen test or multiple marker screening. It is normally offered in the second trimester, usually after the fifteenth week. It is intended as a screening for birth defects, but many women decline to take it because of the high rate of false positive results. A woman pregnant with multiples will produce an abnormal result, due to the increased levels of hormones produced by additional babies. In fact, many spontaneous twin pregnancies are identified in the second trimester after an AFP test returns a positive, or abnormal, result.

The test requires you to have blood drawn, which is sent to a lab to be analyzed. Three components are assessed: alpha-fetoprotein, a substance produced by the fetal liver; human chorionic gonadotropin (HCG), a pregnancy hormone; and unconjugated estriol (uE3), another hormone associated with pregnancy. A quadruple screen may also measure inhipin A, to detect Down syndrome.

Glucose Testing for Gestational Diabetes

Late in the second trimester, you will likely be screened for gestational diabetes. The test measures the amount of glucose in your blood to determine whether pregnancy hormones have affected the way that your body processes insulin. In most cases, the glucose level is assessed via a blood sample. Your doctor will provide you with a sweet, high-glucose beverage and instructions on when to drink it. About an hour later, blood will be drawn and sent to the lab. If your blood serum glucose level is high, you may be at risk for gestational diabetes. Usually a second round of more intensive testing, called an oral glucose tolerance test, is prescribed. You may be required to follow a special diet for a few days, or fast the night before. It can be a time-consuming test, since your blood will be drawn several times.

Amniocentesis (Amnio)

Between the fourteenth and twentieth week of your pregnancy, you may be scheduled for an amniocentesis. During the process of amniocentesis, or amnio, your caregiver uses an ultrasound-guided needle to withdraw fluid from the babies' amniotic sac. Analysis of the fluid sample, which contains fetal cells, provides a wealth of information about the babies.

Amniocentesis may produce some cramping and you'll probably be advised to take it easy after the procedure. There are some inherent risks; the needle's invasion of the uterus can trigger infection, preterm labor, or even miscarriage. In a multiple pregnancy, in which each baby's amniotic sac must be sampled, the risks may be increased. Generally, this procedure is recommended for mothers over the age of thirty-five, or whose families have a history of chromosomal abnormalities or birth defects. It may also be warranted if there is an indication that you will deliver

Mommy Must

In a singleton pregnancy, gestational diabetes screening is usually performed early in the third trimester, but many doctors recommend earlier testing for moms of multiples. The risk of gestational diabetes is nearly doubled for moms expecting more than one baby.

your babies prematurely, as it can be an effective tool for assessing their lung maturity.

Chorionic Villus Sampling (CVS)

An alternative to amniocentesis is chorionic villus sampling (CVS). It is generally performed earlier in pregnancy, even as early as the first trimester. Chorionic villi are tiny tentacles of tissue projecting from the chorion that provide a sample of the babies' genetic material. A catheter is inserted through either the cervix or the abdominal wall to extract a sample of the villi.

Now's the Time to Eat!

With so many facets of a multiple pregnancy beyond your control, your diet is one way that you can directly contribute to your babies' healthy development—what you eat is passed along to the babies through the placenta. It's important not only to eat the right foods, but also to consume enough food to satisfy everyone's nutritional needs.

Mindful Mommy

Although it is an extremely accurate tool for detecting genetic disorders, the risk of miscarriage after CVS is even 1 to 2 percent higher than with amniocentesis. It can be a challenging procedure when there are multiples, especially if they share a placenta. Your doctor will advise you as to the risks and benefits of undergoing such testing.

Plenty of Protein

Research has suggested that protein plays an important role in fetal development. The amino acids found in animal proteins, such as meats, milk, and eggs, are an important component in the creation of human cells. These essential acids cannot be produced by the body but are consumed through the food you eat.

It's recommended that the average woman consume about 10 percent of her calories in protein, or about 50 grams per day. However, a woman expecting multiples needs an increased amount. While you should discuss your specific requirements with your doctor or nutritionist, many experts recommend that expectant mothers of multiples consume 100 to 150 grams of protein daily. Protein is not stored in the body, so it's important to replenish the supply by eating adequate amounts throughout the day, not just at dinner. Here are some protein-rich foods to stock up on:

- Eggs
- Cheese
- Yogurt

Mommy Must

Be careful, though—not all sources of protein are the same. Many sources of animal protein have the disadvantage of being high in fat. It's important to select lean sources of protein. You can also eat a combination of other plant sources of protein to provide the essential acids that your body needs. These include rice and beans, peanut butter, whole grains, and soy.

- Chicken breast
- Fish
- Lean meats such as turkey, ham, or roast beef
- Nuts such as almonds, walnuts, and cashews
- Peanut butter
- Tofu
- Soy milk products
- Beans

Keep Eating Those Carbs

In addition to protein, your body needs an energy boost from complex carbohydrates. Pregnancy is not the time to jump on the low-carb diet bandwagon! Carbohydrates help your body process the extra protein you're consuming and maintain your blood sugar. Just as with protein, it's important to choose the right source of carbohydrates.

There are two types of carbohydrates, simple and complex. Simple carbohydrates give a quick boost of energy from sugar, while complex carbohydrates release energy more slowly over time. Fruit is the preferred source of simple carbohydrates, rather than sugary treats such as candy, cake, or cookies, because of the added vitamins and nutrients it contains. Many fruits also have high water content, so they provide hydration as well as nourishment. Complex carbohydrates are found in many starchy foods, such as bread, cereal, pasta, potatoes, and rice, as well as some vegetables and legumes, such as beans and peas. Choose whole-grain starches for the added fiber they provide. A fiber-rich diet prevents constipation and can reduce your risk of contracting hemorrhoids.

Don't Forget Your Minerals and Vitamins

As you make food choices during your pregnancy, you should consider foods that provide vital minerals such as iron, calcium, and folic acid. While these substances are also available in the form of dietary supplements, you'll give your babies a better start if you ingest them naturally in the foods you eat. Calcium is essential in the creation of your babies' skeletal structure and also enhances heart, muscle, and nerve function. Although the most common source of calcium is dairy products, many green vegetables contain double or triple the amount. Arugula, spinach, and collard greens are excellent sources of calcium.

Many expectant moms of multiples experience anemia due to their increased blood volume during pregnancy. Because iron helps transport oxygen in the blood, it helps combat anemia. The problem with iron intake is that you not only have to take it

Mindful Mommy

Calcium not only helps build your babies' bones and teeth, but it's also been proven to reduce the risk of pregnancy-induced hypertension and preeclampsia. It's good for Mom, too!

in, but your body also has to absorb it properly. Some foods enhance iron absorption and others inhibit it, so food combinations are important. Dairy products, bran cereal, antacids, tea, and soda products can hinder absorption, but waiting about an hour after ingestion to eat iron-rich foods or take an iron supplement will reduce the inhibiting effects. Drinking orange juice may also help, since vitamin C helps convert iron into a form more easily absorbed by the body. Iron-rich foods include:

- Red meats
- Spinach
- Eggs
- Prunes
- Pumpkin seeds
- Soybeans

Folic acid is a B vitamin that is credited for dramatically reducing the risk of birth defects in the brain and spinal cord when taken prior to and during pregnancy. Folate, the natural form of the vitamin, is found in some food sources, such as black beans, asparagus, orange juice, spinach, peanuts, and romaine lettuce. Because of its benefits, some grain products, such as breads, cereals, and pastas, are now enriched with folic acid. However, to ensure that your intake is sufficient, pregnant mothers of multiples should also take a supplement or prenatal multivitamin that includes folic acid.

Nutritional Supplements

In order to obtain maximum nutritional benefits, your doctor may prescribe dietary supplements. Most experts agree that it is easiest for the body to utilize nutrients, vitamins, and minerals when they are obtained through foods, but during a multiple pregnancy, it may be necessary to ingest them in other forms. Your doctor or midwife will be able to advise you on the appropriate dosage and schedule; don't take any vitamins or supplements without consulting a medical professional.

Most women are advised to take a prenatal vitamin daily during their pregnancy, and many begin this regimen even before conception in order to give their baby an optimum start in life. Prenatal vitamin products are specifically designed to provide an extra boost of the vitamins and minerals that are most difficult to obtain through food, while minimizing the elements that can be dangerous to a developing fetus. Regular daily vitamin supplements may be too high in vitamin A, an excess of which has been linked to birth defects, or too low in important nutrients like folic acid and iron.

Many expectant mothers of multiples experience iron deficiency, or anemia. Mothers of multiples are especially susceptible to this condition, so your doctor may routinely recommend an iron supplement in the second or third trimester. It is difficult to obtain sufficient amounts of iron, even with a healthy diet.

If you are underweight, or if you are losing weight due to loss of appetite or nausea, your doctor may advise you to augment your caloric intake with nutritional supplements. These products are available in a variety of flavors, usually in the form of a beverage or pudding snack. They are nutritionally balanced and calorie-dense. If your doctor believes they are appropriate for your situation, he may recommend either a high-protein or high-calorie supplement, or perhaps a combination of both. They are not intended to replace food, but rather to increase your nutritional intake in order to maximize the healthy development of your babies.

Your doctor may also prescribe other supplements, such as calcium, magnesium, zinc, vitamin B, or vitamin D, depending on your individual needs. Of course, you should never take any dietary supplements without discussing them with your physician first. And always follow the recommended dosage amounts. Too much of a good thing is not good!

Drink More! (Water, of course)

Eating right is a good start, but you also have to think about what you drink. Dehydration poses risks to the

Mommy Knows Best

Folic acid, a B vitamin, is essential for the healthy development of a baby's spinal cord and brain. Taken prior to and early in pregnancy, it can help prevent up to 74 percent of neural tube defects, such as spina bifida and anencephaly.

babies, including preterm labor, as well as causing constipation and other complications for mom. Getting your fill of liquids is every bit as important as fueling up on food.

During pregnancy, the blood volume in your body increases, nearly doubling its non-pregnant amount. Your body needs fluid to produce all that extra blood. Thus, good hydration improves your circulation, making you feel better and enhancing the development of your babies. You also require fluid to replenish the amniotic fluid surrounding the babies in your womb. If you're not drinking sufficiently, your body will leach the fluid from other systems. Ultimately, you can end up feeling lethargic, have dry, itchy skin, and become constipated.

Dehydration can also prompt the onset of preterm labor. In fact, rehydration is often one of the first lines of defense against early contractions. You can minimize the risk of preterm labor, and possibly keep yourself out of the hospital, by drinking plenty of fluids.

Most pregnant women are advised to drink six to eight glasses of liquid a day. However, that's if they're having one baby! Moms of multiples should strive for about sixty-four ounces, or about eight eight-ounce glasses. If you find it difficult to fill up on fluid, try these tips and tricks:

- Drink a glass of water before each meal, then refill a glass to sip while you eat.
- Add slices of lemon or lime to flavor plain water.

- Try sparkling waters; the bubbles make them as refreshing as soda.
- Keep a full water bottle next to your bed so that you can sip in the night and first thing in the morning.
- Carry a bottle of water in the car and take a drink at every stoplight.
- Size up: Pour larger glasses or purchase larger bottles.

If you aren't sure whether you're drinking enough, check your urine. The lighter the color of your urine, the more hydrated you are. If it's a dark yellow color, you could be dehydrated.

Stay Active (with Your Dr.'s Advice)

Regular exercise is a vital part of a healthy lifestyle, but during a multiple pregnancy, it can sometimes cause extra stress and strain on your body. You should work with your health-care provider to determine an exercise plan that will incorporate the benefits while minimizing the risks.

Should You Exercise?

If you were active prior to your pregnancy, you may be able to continue your routine. However, pregnancy is not the time to start training for a marathon. Your body is simply too busy building babies to undertake strenuous activity. You should focus your exercise effort on activities that enhance your circulation, strengthen your muscle tone, and help you relax.

Follow your doctor's advice. During the first trimester, you may be able to follow your normal, pre-pregnancy fitness routine, as long as you're aware of your need for extra supplemental calories and hydration. However, as the weeks pass, you will likely be advised to avoid exercise that compromises your pregnancy or puts you at risk for complications. Strenuous exercise can cause you to overheat or become dehydrated. You should avoid any high-impact activity that puts extra pressure on the pelvic floor and can induce preterm labor, such as running or aerobic dancing. Any exercises that strain the abdominal muscles, such as sit-ups or leg lifts, can be damaging during pregnancy. As your uterus grows, your body's center of gravity changes. You may find that your sense of balance is affected, making you unsteady and at higher risk for spills and tumbles.

If you are expecting higher order multiples, exercise may simply be too risky. The combined weight of the babies increases very quickly, making it more difficult for you to move easily. Meanwhile, addi-

Mommy Must

Make sure you're exercising for the right reasons during your pregnancy. Don't let weight management be the motivation behind your workout. This is one time in your life that it is healthy and normal to gain weight! So focus on overall health for you and the babies.

tional exercise may compromise your attempts to sustain high levels of caloric intake, since exercise just burns up calories that would be better applied toward the babies.

Exercise Options

With your doctor's blessing, swimming can be an ideal exercise during your pregnancy. If you have access to a pool, take advantage of it! Swimming provides a cardiovascular workout and feels very refreshing. If swimming laps isn't appealing, consider other water-based exercise options. The buoyancy of the water allows you to move comfortably and reduces strain on your body, creating an optimal exercise environment for a pregnant woman.

Walking is another excellent exercise option. It's free, doesn't require any special equipment, and is easily accessible. You can set your own pace and adjust your level of intensity according to how you're feeling. You can walk outside in fair weather, or head inside to a shopping mall when it's too hot, too cold, or rainy.

Gentle stretching exercises are also beneficial. Pregnancy yoga classes are available in many locations. The mental relaxation fostered by yoga can be especially soothing. Of course, check with your doctor before participating in a yoga routine, and ensure that the class instructor is fully qualified. To find a good class in your area, inquire at the hospital where you plan to deliver or check with your local mothers of multiples organization.

What to Avoid

While there are certain things that you can do to enhance your health during pregnancy, there are many things that you should *not* do in order to assure the safety of your developing babies. Certainly, there are some activities, such as excessive drinking and smoking, that are inadvisable at any time, but the potential harm to two, three, or more developing individuals makes these actions inexcusable during pregnancy. However, other seemingly harmless things that were part of your life before you were pregnant may pose a danger now that you are expecting twins or more.

For example, soaking in a hot tub should be avoided during pregnancy. Studies have shown a connection between hot tub use and miscarriage in the first trimester. In addition, soaking in a 100-plus-degree hot tub can cause a body's internal thermostat to rise and overheat, a dangerous condition for the fetuses.

That morning jolt of caffeine from coffee may be a cherished routine when you're not pregnant, but you may want to consider cutting back or going

Mindful Mommy

With any exercise program, be sure to wear supportive clothing and proper footwear. Your feet will swell and enlarge during pregnancy; you may have to invest in a larger pair of sneakers!

without while you are. Although moderate amounts of caffeine aren't necessarily harmful, studies have shown an association with stillbirth, birth defects, and other complications. Caffeine, found in coffee, some teas, and some sodas, stimulates your heart rate and metabolism. That can put stress on your body, and your babies. Your doctor can advise you as to how much is too much.

Medications and Herbs

The shelves of pharmacies overflow with over-the-counter medications and remedies for every known condition. Usually you wouldn't think twice about taking aspirin for a headache or a decongestant for a cold. However, you would never give these drugs to an infant, which is basically what you're doing when you take medications during your pregnancy. Any over-the-counter drugs should be approved by your doctor. If you are taking prescription drugs, your health-care provider will review your situation and make a recommendation as to whether it is safe to continue their use during pregnancy.

The popularity of herbal remedies to treat common ailments has risen in recent years. Be wary about

Mommy Must

Caffeine can hamper your ability to absorb iron by as much as 40 percent if you drink a caffeinated beverage within one hour of a meal. That's a factor worth considering when you're already at risk for iron deficiency.

their use during your pregnancy; you're not only administering them to yourself, but they will also impact your babies' well-being. Don't be misled into thinking that "natural" or nonmedical approaches are necessarily neutral; they may have harmful consequences. Always consult a medical provider before taking any kind of herbal product, including herbal teas, when you're pregnant.

Unsafe Foods

Listeriosis is an infection caused by eating foods that contain the *listeria* bacteria. It's not a terribly dangerous condition for most adults, but can have devastating effects on fetuses or newborns. You can reduce your risk of contracting such an infection by avoiding certain foods. Soft cheeses, including Brie, Camembert, feta, Roquefort, and asadero, should only be eaten if they have been cooked by boiling or broiling until they are bubbly. You can also minimize your risk by properly handling other foods that are likely to be contaminated with listeria. These include any foods that have been precooked and then refrigerated, such as hot dogs or deli-style luncheon meats. Cooking these foods will kill the bacteria, so they are safe to eat after they have been thoroughly reheated.

Despite its reputation as a delicious source of nutrition, some seafood is also potentially dangerous during pregnancy with multiples. Toxic levels of methyl mercury can be found in some types of predator fish, including shark, swordfish, tile fish, and king mackerel. Mercury can damage the developing fetuses' nervous system. That doesn't mean that you can't enjoy seafood while you're pregnant. Check with your doctor about the types of fish to avoid, and enjoy other varieties in moderation.

Cat Litter

You don't have to give up your kitty while you're expecting, but stay away from the litter box. Toxoplasmosis is a parasite that can be contained in cat waste. If you have a cat, you may already have been exposed to it, and it's not harmful to most adults. But it can cause health problems for unborn babies, so you want to limit your exposure.

Handling your cat won't bring you in contact with the parasite, but you should avoid coming in contact with feline feces. Have someone else clean the litter box while you're pregnant to minimize the risk. It's not likely to be a chore that you relish doing anyway!

Secondhand Smoke

Even if you don't smoke, the dangerous effects of tobacco can still impact your babies. Secondhand smoke, which is also known as passive smoke, is the

Mindful Mommy

About one-third of all cases of listeriosis occur in pregnant women. They are particularly susceptible because pregnancy hormones cause changes to their immune system. Women who are pregnant are about twenty times more likely to contract the disease.

combination of exhalations from a smoker and smoke from their burning cigarettes, and it can be harmful to developing fetuses. Babies exposed to secondhand smoke are smaller and more likely to be born prematurely; with your multiples already at risk for these conditions, you don't want to heighten the odds. Passive smoke increases the risk of asthma and cancer, and children of smokers often exhibit increased irritability.

Stay away from smokers while you're pregnant. Keep your home smoke-free; if you have family members who smoke, ask them not to smoke inside while you're pregnant. (Better yet, ask them to stop altogether!) Avoid the smoking section of public places such as restaurants and shopping centers.

Chapter 5

It's Their Birth Day!

AFTER THE LONG MONTHS of pregnancy, the onset of labor is the transition time marking the departure of pregnancy and the arrival of your babies. Whether your labor is long or short, weeks early or days over-due, it's an important process. It's the work your body must do to bring your babies to life.

Ready to Labor?

The process of childbirth can be broken down into three stages: labor, pushing and delivery of the placenta(s). Labor is generally the longest and most uncomfortable stage, during which the cervix must fully open as a passageway for the babies. The good news about labor with multiples is that the hard work accomplished by the body during this stage accom-modates both (or all) babies; you don't have to repeat this stage for each baby.

There are three phases of labor. Early, or latent, labor is the first phase of the first stage of labor, when the cervix prepares to open and provide access for the babies' departure from the womb. This readying of the cervix is called ripening, and it requires the cervix to do two things: efface (thin out) and dilate (open). You can be in early labor for several days, or even weeks, without really being aware of it. Gentle contractions and pressure on the cervix open it a couple of centimeters. They may be as infrequent as once an hour, but will occur with increasing frequency and will intensify as the phase progresses. They can last as long as forty-five seconds each. Most women are fairly comfortable through this stage, and are able to participate in light activity.

Early labor gives way to the active phase when the contractions are about five minutes apart and the cervix has dilated to three or four centimeters. While it may have taken twelve hours for the cervix to dilate a couple of centimeters during the latent phase, the increased contractions and pressure of the first baby moving toward the birth canal speed up the process during active labor. It can take only a few hours or as little as fifteen minutes for the cervix to fully dilate to ten centimeters.

Mindful Mommy

Latent labor lasts, on average, for ten to twelve hours. For women experiencing childbirth for the first time, it can be longer. However, the extra weight and pressure associated with carrying two or more babies often expedites the process for mothers of multiples.

Just when you think that you can't take any more, the final phase of labor intensifies your discomfort. Contractions lasting more than a minute come fast and furious, as frequently as every other minute. The presenting baby's proximity to your fully dilated cervix places increasing pressure on your bottom. You may feel like you want to push, but will have to focus your energy on resisting the urge, according to your doctor's or midwife's direction. To make matters worse, your body may betray you, compounding your discomfort with nausea, vomiting, and pressure in your rectum.

In the midst of this discomfort, you will likely be moved to an operating room or a delivery room equipped for emergency surgery. That's a good sign; it means that the arrival of your babies is not far away!

How Do Your Babies Present Themselves?

An important factor in delivering multiples is presentation, the term used to describe the position of the babies within the womb. The presentation of the babies at the time of delivery will guide your doctors in deciding the best method of delivery. There are several combinations of positions that your babies can take (see the following page).

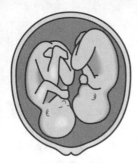

Vertex / Vertex

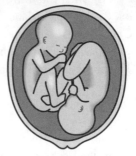

Vertex / Breech

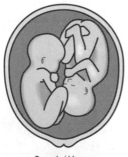

Breech / Vertex

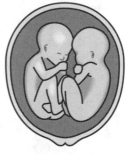

Breech / Breech

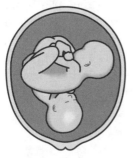

Vertex / Transverse

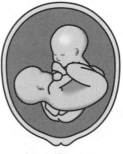

Breech / Transverse

Vertex Babies

Vertex is the term to describe a baby that is resting head-down, the most common and safest option for vaginal delivery. Your doctor will be most concerned with whether the presenting baby—that is, the one closest to the cervix—is vertex, as this is the baby that would enter the birth canal first. A twin pregnancy where both babies are vertex is the best candidate for a vaginal birth.

Breech Babies

A breech baby is the opposite of a vertex baby; his head is pointing upright. A breech baby may be arranged in one of three ways:

Frank breech: The buttocks are positioned closest to the cervix, with the legs folded straight up toward the head.

Complete breech: The buttocks are pointed toward the cervix, but the arms and legs are crossed in front of the body.

Incomplete or footling breech: One or both legs are dangling down toward the cervix.

It is only rarely favorable to deliver vaginally if the presenting baby is breech. However, a breech baby following a vertex twin may be a candidate for vaginal delivery. Sometimes the doctor or midwife will make an attempt to turn the breech baby. If unsuccessful, consideration will be given to the baby's status. Is he tolerating the labor well? Does he appear to be in any distress? Is he frank breech, the least difficult position to deliver? Fetal monitoring and ultrasound will give a picture of the baby's condition.

One of the most important criteria to consider in determining whether a baby should be delivered breech is how her size compares to her co-twin. If the second baby is smaller than the first, she is more likely to be a successful breech delivery, as the doctor can be fairly assured that she will pass through the birth canal. Your doctor's previous experience will determine his comfort level with breech delivery.

Transverse Babies

Transverse babies rest horizontally in the womb. A transverse baby lying at the bottom of the womb is not a good candidate for a vaginal delivery. Usually, however, the baby closest to the cervix is either breech or vertex and the second baby rests in a transverse position higher in the womb, close to the mother's rib cage. Your doctor will most likely base a delivery decision on the position of the presenting baby.

Mindful Mommy

Even identical twins can look very different at birth when one is vertex and the other is delivered breech. A vertex baby's head is rounded by its headfirst passage through the birth canal, while a breech baby's head is more pointy and cone-shaped. After birth, the soft skull tissue reforms into a normal shape and they will look more alike.

Exit Options:
Vaginal Birth or Cesarean

Delivery through the birth canal and out the vagina is generally the safest method of birth for mother and babies, and therefore it is the preferred approach, unless certain circumstances create risks that make a cesarean section a better option. Vaginal delivery carries less risk of hemorrhage or infection, requires less anesthesia, and has a quicker recovery time. It also produces less scarring.

Vaginal delivery is not an option if

- You are having triplets, quadruplets, or other higher order multiples.
- Your twins are monoamniotic (share an amniotic sac).
- The presentation of either baby is transverse lie.
- You have active genital herpes.
- You have placenta previa or another medical condition.
- Your pelvic structure makes it difficult for your babies to pass through.

Mommy Knows Best

The babies may also benefit from a vaginal delivery. As they travel through the birth canal, their lungs are compressed, forcing out fluid and preparing them to breathe air.

Vaginal delivery may be discouraged if:

- One or both babies is breech.
- You have preeclampsia.
- One or more of the babies are in severe distress and cannot tolerate labor.
- Previous cesarean delivery or abdominal surgery puts you at risk for uterine rupture.

Vaginal Birth After Cesarean (VBAC)

At one time, a previous cesarean section automatically ruled out a vaginal delivery. That is not the case these days, however. The danger of labor and delivery after cesarean surgery is that the incision site could rupture. New techniques make that less likely now. Most doctors are willing to attempt a VBAC (short for vaginal birth after cesarean), as long as certain conditions are met.

It's important for your doctor or midwife to review your case if you have had a previous c-section, so be sure they are aware of your history. While in most cases a VBAC is feasible, the extra strain that multiples place on your uterus may make it too risky.

Push, Push, Push!

The process of labor prepares the mother's body for a vaginal delivery. After the first stage of labor completely opens the cervix to provide a gateway for the baby's exit from the womb, it's time for the second stage of labor: pushing the presenting baby through the pelvic bones and out the vaginal opening. This stage can last for five minutes or several hours. Usually, it lasts about an hour. On average, it takes three to five pushes to move the baby out.

While the contractions may subside somewhat in frequency, they won't lessen in intensity, and they will be accompanied by an overwhelming urge to push or bear down. Your doctor or midwife may guide you to coordinate your pushing efforts with your contractions, or you may be encouraged to bear down when it feels right. If you received an epidural for pain management, your sensation may be dulled and you should probably receive some coaching.

The force of your uterus's contractions will continue to compel the baby through your pelvis toward the vaginal opening. If necessary, an episiotomy will be performed to prevent tearing of the perineum. The doctor will make a small cut to the tissue that stretches between your vagina and rectum. The clean cut heals faster than ripped tissue. Or perineal massage may help stretch the tissue to accommodate the oncoming baby.

Mommy Must

The bad news: You have to experience this stage of labor separately with each baby. The good news: Twins are usually a bit smaller than singleton babies and most mothers of multiples don't have a difficult time pushing them out.

Once the head crowns, or bulges through the perineum, the excitement begins. Your doctor or midwife will slowly coach the first baby's head out of your vagina. You may be instructed to stop pushing while her nose and mouth are suctioned. After the head, the largest part of the baby's body, has exited, the arms, torso, and legs slip out without much exertion. The umbilical cord will be clamped and cut, and your first twin will be handed off to a waiting attendant.

It's done! The first baby has arrived! You can bask in the joy of this moment and relax for a few moments. You're not completely finished yet, though. There's more to come.

The Intermission: Between Babies

If you were having a singleton, your childbirth experience would end here. But you're having another baby! While twins may be born within a few minutes of each other, most arrive at intervals of twenty to thirty minutes. This intermission between babies is a crucial time, during which both babies' condition will be assessed.

With more room to move, the second baby may stretch out and change position—with luck, into a vertex presentation. His rearrangement will likely be monitored by ultrasound to determine the course of action. If the baby is in a breech or transverse position, your doctor may attempt to turn him. This process, called external cephalic version, can be uncomfortable, as the doctor pushes forcefully on your abdomen in an attempt to turn the baby head down.

This baby requires some careful monitoring during this time. If his bag of water remained intact during the delivery of his co-twin, it will need to be broken now. With his brother or sister out of the way, his situation poses some risk. The previous contractions and pushing activity may have caused the placenta to detach, reducing the amount of oxygen delivered to the remaining baby. And there is always a concern about cord compression or prolapse, if the umbilical cord enters the birth canal before the baby does.

Your contractions will also be watched carefully during this time. If your uterus slacks off, you may be given a drug to reactivate the contractions to deliver the second baby. With a path already paved by her co-twin, the good news is that the second twin usually requires fewer pushes and is often born relatively quickly.

And You're Still Not Done Yet

After both babies are delivered, there's one final step. You have to deliver the placenta(s). This important organ has been the source of nutrition and

Mindful Mommy

There have been some cases where twins or other multiples experience an extended intermission between births. Usually this occurs when preterm labor cannot be halted and one multiple is delivered extremely prematurely.

nourishment for your babies for the last few months, but now that it is no longer needed, it is time for it to depart your womb.

Your contractions will continue, with a different purpose. Instead of dilating your cervix or forcing out a baby, these contractions serve to separate the placenta from the uterine wall. A final push will expel it through your vagina. Fused or single placentas will be delivered in one shot. If your babies had separate placentas, you may have to go through this process more than once.

When the doctor or midwife clamps each cord, request that they distinguish the cords—and the corresponding placentas—so that they can be identified for ownership. In the event that there is a problem with one of the babies, an examination of cord or placental abnormalities might help pinpoint a diagnosis.

With your hard work done, you can lie back and relax. If you were given an episiotomy or experienced any tearing, you'll be stitched up and cleaned up. Your epidural may be removed at this time if you don't require any follow-up care.

Mommy Must

Most hospitals do so as a matter of routine, but you'll want the placenta(s) sent to pathology for examination. An analysis may reveal your babies' zygosity. A monochorionic placenta will indicate that your twins are monozygotic, or identical.

A Section About C-Sections

Nearly all triplets, quadruplets, and higher order multiples are delivered by cesarean section. About 50 percent of twin pregnancies are candidates for cesarean delivery. Your cesarean delivery may not be a surprise. With multiples, it is often a planned event, decided in advance based on your situation. Even if you prefer a vaginal delivery, you should consider the possibility of a c-section and prepare accordingly.

The Surgery Itself

Fortunately, the procedure itself is relatively short. The doctor will make an incision low across the pubic area; this "bikini cut" creates a less conspicuous scar and reduces the risk of uterine complications in future pregnancies. After cutting through muscle and tissue to access the uterus, the doctor will make an incision through the uterine wall to access the first baby. As the baby is lifted out, you may feel some pressure and tugging, but no pain.

As the baby is lifted out, ask to have the screen lowered so that you can have a look. The baby's cord will

Mommy Knows Best

During pregnancy, babies are often identified as "Baby A," "Baby B," "Baby C," and so forth based on their presentation, with the baby closest to the cervix termed Baby A. In a cesarean delivery, the babies may or may not arrive in order, depending on how they are arranged in the womb. The baby closest to the incision will be the first to be born.

be clamped and cut, and the baby will be handed to an attendant for examination. In the meantime, the doctor will already be moving on to the next baby, reaching into your uterus and pulling out another multiple. Another attendant will be ready to receive her, and the process will continue until all the babies have been delivered. You may be able to hear your babies cry out as they take their first breaths. Your partner may have the opportunity to participate in the process, cutting the cords or holding the babies after they have been examined.

After the babies are removed from your womb, your doctor will deliver the placenta(s) and examine your uterus for fragments of placental tissue. You may be given medication in your IV to help your overworked uterus start the road to recovery. Then the process of suturing and stitching begins, which often takes longer than the actual delivery.

Emergency C-Section Combination Birth

Many mothers are very concerned about the prospect of delivering their first baby vaginally and then having a c-section to deliver the second baby, as it means experiencing the worst sensations of both methods: suffering through the discomfort of labor as well as surgery, and having to recover from both an episiotomy and an incision. While you'll probably hear plenty of stories about this unfortunate series of events in twin birth, statistically it's not likely to happen. Only 15 percent of twin births happen in this fashion.

No doctor prefers this combined method of delivery. If there is any doubt that the second baby can be delivered vaginally, a cesarean section would be recommended to begin with. Surgery to deliver the second baby is only performed when fetal distress is indicated and the baby's life is at risk. Although it is not the ideal experience, most mothers would agree that their baby's life is worth the added discomfort.

Those First Few Moments

No matter how you deliver, your babies will spend their first few moments amid a whirlwind of activity. Most deliveries of twins or more will be attended by an array of medical staff. Often the babies are well outnumbered by their attendants, with at least one doctor and nurse caring for each infant. Immediately after birth, your babies' condition will be assessed. After placing them on a warming tray and cleaning them up, the medical staff will be checking out several different aspects of their physical state.

In addition, your babies will be weighed and measured. Ointment or eye drops will be placed in their

Mindful Mommy

Your babies' first standardized test is the Apgar, which provides a general assessment of their health at birth. Apgar is assessed twice, when they are one minute old and then again, five minutes later. A score of ten is perfect, and anything above seven is considered average. If there is cause for concern based on a lower score, your baby will be treated according to his needs.

eyes. Their footprints will be inked, and a blood sample will be taken for testing. They'll be given a dose of vitamin K to assist with blood clotting. Depending on their condition, as well as your recovery status, the babies may spend some time in your arms. This quiet period of alertness that follows birth is an ideal time to initiate breastfeeding.

If your babies are born early, the events of their birth may be surrounded by a bit more concern and immediacy. Neonatologists will be standing by to care for them as they make their entry. Quick action will be taken to ease their transition from the womb to the world, especially to help them breathe. They may be whisked away to the NICU (neonatal intensive care unit), and your opportunity to spend time with them may be limited as the medical staff strives to stabilize them.

The abrupt end to your pregnancy can be a very difficult experience. Your babies may be facing several months of critical care. However, many premature infants survive their ominous start in life; only time will tell your babies' stories. Have faith in the medical staff's ability to care for them and in your love for your little ones!

On the Road to Recovery

Just as your body—and mind—took some time to adjust to the idea of being pregnant, you'll need some time to recover after giving birth. Your recovery period will be determined by how you delivered; cesarean moms have undergone major surgery and will need more time to heal, although a vaginal delivery also takes a toll on a woman's body.

After Vaginal Delivery

After delivery, your uterus will begin to shrink back to its pre-pregnancy size. You may feel some mild cramping during this process, but you should not experience extreme discomfort. If you do, notify your doctor. You'll have some bleeding, which may be heavy at first. For the first few days you may find that you soak a sanitary napkin in a couple of hours. If you've had a previous pregnancy, you won't find this surprising, but it may be heavier than you experienced in the past. That's because your uterus stretched and expanded further to accommodate the extra babies. The bloody discharge, called lochia, can last for several weeks after delivery. It should taper off, however, and should not include any large clumps or clots. If it increases, or is accompanied by pain, fever, or a foul odor, notify your doctor right away.

You will need to wear sanitary napkins to accommodate this discharge for up to six weeks after you deliver. Tampons are not recommended. If you experienced anemia during your pregnancy, it's important to continue supplementing your iron intake, either by eating iron-rich foods or by taking pills prescribed by your doctor.

Although you'll probably be ready to leave the hospital soon after your delivery, it will take a couple of weeks for your body to return to full strength. After the strain of pregnancy, the process of labor is intense—your body worked hard!—and you need to give yourself time to recuperate. It's not realistic to expect that you will get plenty of rest and relaxation; the weeks following the delivery of multiples are hectic, to say the least. But you should definitely consider lining up plenty of help so that you can minimize your responsibilities and focus your energy exclusively on caring for yourself and the babies.

After C-Section

A cesarean section is major surgery, and necessitates more intensive recovery. You'll probably have to remain in bed for at least twelve hours, after which time you'll be encouraged to move around or at least get out of bed. It may be unpleasant; the effects of the surgery and the anesthesia may leave you feeling like you've been hit by a truck. Rely on the nurses and caregivers to assist you. You may have a great deal of pain or discomfort, but relief is available. Discuss your options for pain medication with your doctor.

Mindful Mommy

If you had an episiotomy or any tearing of the perineum during your delivery, you may be somewhat sore. Ice packs, sitz baths, and witch-hazel pads can relieve the discomfort. You may also be plagued by hemorrhoids as your distended veins return to normal capacity. Discuss their treatment with your caregiver.

A cesarean section does not exempt you from the other aftereffects of delivering a baby. You will still have some cramping as your uterus returns to its normal size, and you will have a vaginal discharge of lochia as your body expels blood and tissue. As with a vaginal delivery, you'll have to wear sanitary napkins for several weeks after your babies are born.

As you recover from a c-section, you'll have to avoid strenuous activity for a period of time. That may include driving, stair climbing, and heavy lifting. Depending on your circumstances, it may be difficult to obey some of these restrictions. However, it is important to follow your doctor's recommendations during your recovery. You cannot effectively care for your newborns if you are unwell. Arrange for extra help and give your body the time and nurturing it needs to heal.

Emotional Impact

No matter how much you read, study, and prepare for the arrival of your babies, their birth will be nothing like you expected. You may feel overwhelmed by emotions: relief, anxiety, elation, despair, fear,

Mindful Mommy

You can still initiate breastfeeding, even if you are taking pain medication. You doctor will advise you if the medication will impact the babies. Even if it prevents you from feeding the babies, you can still begin the nursing process using a pump.

and love. Your conflicting feelings may stir up some unusual reactions. Remember that this is a time of transition. You're not pregnant with multiples any more; rather, you are the mother of two, three, or more infants. You are all settling into your new roles as a family and will require some time to adjust.

Postpartum depression (PPD) is characterized by feelings of hopelessness that last most of the day, and don't diminish after several weeks. It's normal to feel overwhelmed or out of control, but you need to seek medical attention if your feelings are preventing you from properly caring for your babies or yourself.

Have some strategies in place for coping with the stress of multiples. Line up plenty of help to see you through the rough times. Maintain a sense of humor. Find the joy in your amazing babies. Establish priorities and give yourself permission to temporarily release any nonessential responsibilities.

Communication is key. Talk to your spouse or partner about your feelings. Share your experience with fellow parents of multiples; they will understand what you're going through. Down the road, you will recall the rush of emotion that followed the birth of your babies with amazing tenderness.

Mindful Mommy

Fifteen percent of women experience postpartum depression after giving birth, and mothers of twins or more are particularly at risk. A 2004 study by the National Organization of Mothers of Twins Clubs found that nearly 40 percent of moms of multiples experienced depression.

Chapter 6

Embrace Your New Life

THERE'S NO DOUBT THAT having multiples will change your life forever. But how will they impact your lifestyle, the day-to-day routines of work, play, and home? Will the babies slide right into your family's existing schedule, or do you need to make some changes to accommodate their arrival? As you anticipate some of the ways that twins will impact your relationships and activities, you'll be better equipped to anticipate any necessary adjustments and make a smooth transition into your new lifestyle.

New Cost Concerns

Your financial situation will surely be affected. From medical bills to dual college savings plans, the costs of raising simultaneous siblings can be exorbitant. Careful financial planning is crucial to surviving without breaking the bank.

Income Versus Expenses

To establish a workable budget, start with your assets. What income is available for spending? If you're used to being a two-income family, consider the impact of the pregnancy and impending birth on Mom's earning status. Does she stand to lose money due to pregnancy bed rest, childbirth, or maternity leave? Will she return to work after the babies arrive? Will Dad need to take any extended leave?

After evaluating your income, make a list of expense categories, such as housing, utilities, food, transportation, insurance, entertainment, and clothing. Identify categories in three ways: fixed (payment due every month at the same time), flexible (varying in amount), or periodic (paid quarterly or annually). Using past bills and statements, generate an estimate of how much you historically spend on each category.

Now list your anticipated expenses or increases due to multiples: furnishings, equipment, child care, medical bills, diapers, formula (if bottle-feeding), clothing, etc. Estimate how much you'll need to spend for each item. It's not an exact science; just a small amount of research will give you enough

Mindful Mommy

Some companies offer discounts or incentive programs for families with multiples and it is well worth your time to investigate them. In most cases, you'll be required to write a letter and furnish copies of the babies' birth certificates. For more information, search the Internet for "multiple birth discount program" or check with your local parents of multiples organization.

information to craft a reasonable guess. Compare your income to your expenses. If they're basically equivalent, or if your income exceeds your expenses, you're in good shape. But if you're like most people, your expenses far outweigh your income.

Making Ends Meet

Sometimes you're forced into making a choice: increase your income or reduce your expenses. You can accomplish the first option by taking out loans, by earning a return on investments, or by someone changing jobs or adding a job. It's generally easier and less risky to attempt the second option, reducing expenses.

There are several ways to reduce expenses. Some of them may dwindle naturally due to your lifestyle change after having multiples. For example, you may find that you spend a lot less on entertainment and travel because you don't go out as often while your multiples are young. But in some areas it may require some conscious action to cut back, perhaps by clipping coupons, switching to lower cost services, or cutting out nonessentials.

If the basis of your financial concern is centered around spending on the babies, take heart. There are many strategies for obtaining the items you need at a discount. For starters, there is a tremendous market for used baby equipment, especially among your fellow families with multiples. Network with your local parents of multiples organization to find great buys on used strollers, highchairs, cribs, and everything else you'll need. Thrift stores and consignment shops are also good sources for baby bargains.

In addition, you're likely to be the beneficiary of generous gifts from family and friends. People love to buy for babies, especially when there's more than one. If you are having a baby shower, be politely specific about your needs, and chances are they'll be met.

To Work or Not to Work?

Unless you've won the lottery or have a money tree growing in the backyard, someone in the family is going to have to generate some income to pay the bills. Since it's going to be a good eighteen years before your multiples are able to earn their keep, that someone is likely to be one or both parents. One of the biggest decisions that parents will have to confront is the issue of working versus staying at home to care for the new arrivals. Basically it boils down to this: give up a paycheck, or pay someone else to care for your babies.

For some families, the choice, one way or the other, is clear. Your financial requirements may demand a dual income to survive. Or perhaps staying at home is the fulfillment of a long-sought dream. But other families face some heavy-duty soul searching and number crunching to reach a solution.

Making the Decision

There are many factors to consider in making the decision, among them career impact, child-care options, parenting philosophy, and expenses. It may be helpful to sit down with your partner and make some notes. Sort out your feelings and discuss any anxieties. Weigh the pros and cons of each option and compare the consequences. Examine the long-term and the short-term benefits of each approach. Both parents should evaluate their earning ability, potential benefits such as health insurance, and their personal goals and desires. Then you'll be able to make a joint decision that will benefit the entire family.

If you are conflicted about this decision, there are some alternative work options that can give you the best of both worlds. Flexible scheduling, job sharing, or working from home are some of the ways that you can generate an income while maximizing your time as a caregiver. If your existing employer isn't willing to explore these options, it may be a good time to consider a career change.

If you decide to stay home and this will be a new role for you, you may be concerned about your chang-

Mommy Must

The Family and Medical Leave Act allows both mothers and fathers to take a total of twelve work weeks of unpaid leave during any twelve-month period. It is a particularly welcome benefit for parents of multiples during those busy months with newborns. To find out if you are eligible, visit the U.S. Department of Labor's Web site at www.dol.gov/esa/whd/fmla/.

ing identity. Rest assured that like any job, although it has its moments of frustration and drudgery, it is also tremendously rewarding. For your twins or more, it's a once-in-a-lifetime opportunity—their lifetime, that is. You can never return to the precious early years of their infancy and babyhood, and they pass by very quickly. Enjoy the opportunity while it lasts.

Multiples Can Rock Your Relationship Boat

Many parents acknowledge that the experience of having multiples is a true test of their relationship. After the earthquake of multiples rocks your world, there are bound to be some aftershocks, and many times they are felt between husband and wife. Amid the endless cycle of crying, feeding, and diapering babies, it can be very difficult to make your marriage a priority. Remember, however, that sustaining your relationship as a couple is an important part of keeping your family strong. Put your marriage into a long-term perspective and don't get bogged down by the short-term demands of your babies.

Despite the changes that multiples bring to your life, many of your physical and emotional needs will remain the same. Use constructive communication to express your needs and desires. Perhaps you want your husband to show that he appreciates you. Or maybe you'd like your wife to acknowledge your help more often.

In order to make your marriage a priority, you're going to have to invest some time in it, and not just a rushed minute here and there as you hand off baby duties. Schedule time together as you would any other appointment. It could be a lunch date during a workday, or an evening out while a sitter keeps the babies. Then use that time wisely and enjoy each other. Don't turn it into a complaining session where you find fault with one another. Remember why you married each other in the first place!

Defining Dad's Role

(Okay, Mommy—bookmark this page and hand over the book to Dad. But even though this section is for him, you should read it too to get an idea of what he's going through!)

New fathers of multiples may feel overlooked when so much attention is heaped on the mother during the pregnancy and the babies after the birth. It's easy to feel lost in the shuffle. In fact, a typical male reaction is to withdraw from the situation. However, this is the time to overcome your instincts and remember that this is not an experience that is only happening to your partner; as the father of multiples, enjoy your chance to equally share in the joys and frustrations of the babies' care.

During the pregnancy, the mother retains most of the physical control of the babies' nurturing and growth. That doesn't exclude fathers as an active participant. Through your support of their mother, you are giving your babies the best possible start in life. Make it your goal to nurture your wife. Prepare healthy snacks for her, bring her a glass of water, and encourage her to rest up as much as possible. If your physician recommends bed rest during the pregnancy, it will likely fall to you to pick up the pieces on the home front, fulfilling the obligations that she would normally carry out.

Emotional Support

In addition to physical support, you play an important emotional role. Worries about coping with pregnancy complications, labor, breastfeeding, and managing infant multiples loom large in the mind of an expectant mother. Hormonal fluctuations and the physical impact of pregnancy on a mother's body intensify her emotions. Your positive and upbeat attitude will go a long way toward reducing stress and dispelling your partner's anxieties. Educate yourself to prepare for the challenges ahead; talk to other fathers about their experiences, read books about multiples (such as this one), and investigate Internet resources (see Appendix A for a list of helpful sites).

Mindful Mommy

As a dad of twins, you're in good company. Many well-known leaders, actors, writers, and sports figures have fathered multiples. For example, William Shakespeare had fraternal twins. Mohammed Ali is the father of twin daughters, as was Nat King Cole. Actors Mel Gibson, Robert De Niro, and Jimmy Stewart all fathered twins.

Going along to doctor appointments and checkups will be a reassuring experience for both of you.

The good news about being a father of twins or more is that you have the opportunity to be more fully involved in their care than a father of singletons might. You have an important extra set of hands that will be much in demand. The bad news is that you *have* to be fully involved in their care. With extra mouths to feed and bottoms to diaper, there is never a lack of work to be done. Find a niche, a chore that you can master, such as preparing the day's bottles, bathing the babies, or doing the laundry, and then take responsibility for that activity without having to be asked.

Above all, in the midst of the chaos and confusion, help your partner to keep things in perspective. The hectic pace of managing newborn multiples is temporary; life will eventually resume a semblance of normality.

Your Other Children . . .

If you already have other children, you may be concerned about how the arrival of twins or more will impact them. There's no way around it; there are some changes in store. It's important to properly prepare them for their new role as big brother or sister of multiples.

Educate and involve your children from the beginning. Introduce them to twinning concepts, and update them on the babies' development throughout the pregnancy. Once the babies arrive, identify specific, age-appropriate ways that they can help their younger siblings. Even toddlers can contribute by fetching supplies!

Meeting Siblings' Needs

As you prepare for your multiples, also consider your child-care needs for your other children. You may have to provide alternative care for them in the event of bed rest or hospitalization during pregnancy. Designate a caregiver in advance, and inform your children of the plans beforehand so that they are familiar and comfortable with the situation.

Your older children may feel displaced or overlooked when the new arrivals come on the scene. Assuage their distress by planning some special surprises that focus attention on them and their importance as "big" brothers or sisters. Stash away some toys or gifts to present at opportune moments, especially items that can keep them quietly occupied when you're busy with the babies. More than

Mommy Knows Best

The same goes for their arrangements during delivery. Having a trusted friend or grandparent available to help care for siblings allows you to focus on the newborns.

gifts, they'll likely crave your time and undivided attention, so make it a priority to preserve cherished routines that provide an opportunity for one-on-one time, such as a morning snuggle, after-school chat, or bedtime story.

Mommy's Stress Management

Families experience stress for many reasons, but having multiples generates a unique combination of physical and emotional strain that can push many people to the breaking point. Equipping yourself with coping strategies is one of the best ways to prepare yourself for the challenges ahead, and can help diffuse stress before it builds to a crescendo.

In many cases, the stress begins in pregnancy, with anxiety about medical risks and an unknown future. Don't let your worries cast a negative shadow over your pregnancy experience. Keep a positive outlook. Talk to other multiple birth families about their experiences. You'll notice that, in most cases, everything turned out fine. Everyone survived and is thriving.

If you are a spiritual person, you will likely find great reassurance in practicing your faith. Many families find that prayer and meditation not only calm their anxieties, but also have a positive impact on their well-being—and the babies', as well. Relying on a higher power can carry you through the times when your life seems out of control.

Once the babies are born, the stress continues. Lack of sleep, hormonal fluctuations, and the constant demands of baby care culminate to produce stressed-out parents. It's important to remember that the situation is temporary. "This **two** shall pass" is a favorite mantra of twin parents.

Chapter 7

The First Few Months: Crazy Daze

INTRODUCING TWINS, TRIPLETS, OR more into a family demands some adjustment from everyone involved. The new babies are getting used to breathing, eating, and sleeping. The parents are juggling their work and home responsibilities while trying to meet the needs of two or more infants. Older siblings have to get used to sharing the spotlight with the new additions. Even the family pet has to adjust to the new smells, sounds, and schedules.

Sleep Solutions

What's the hardest thing about having newborn multiples? Ask any parent, and you'll likely hear a common lament: lack of sleep. With babies that need to eat every two to three hours around the clock, parents' normal nighttime sleep routine is out the window. Rather than retiring at 10:00 p.m. and rising refreshed at 7:00 a.m., they find themselves dozing for an hour in between feedings at 3:00 a.m., and catching a catnap at 3:00 p.m.

How Babies Sleep

Newborns need a lot of sleep. Unfortunately, the sleep patterns of young infants aren't concentrated during the nighttime hours, like adults'. Throughout a twenty-four hour cycle, babies sleep, wake up to eat, and return to sleep several times. As they grow older, they'll start to extend the amount of time between feedings, and thus stay asleep for longer periods of time. But in the meantime, parents have to adjust to a schedule of sleeping in short intervals.

Most full-term, normal birth weight newborns require between sixteen and eighteen hours of sleep a day. During the first few weeks, that time is spread throughout the day and night, in two- to three-hour bursts. Singleton parents can focus their attention on the baby when he awakes, then return to sleep when he does. The challenge for parents of multiples is that their babies' sleep patterns may not coincide, greatly reducing the amount of available rest periods in between feedings. In addition, multiples tend to

Mommy Knows Best

Remember that infancy is temporary and fleeting. Your babies will grow older and stronger and they WILL sleep through the night. Rest assured that the day will eventually arrive, and take comfort in realizing that every new dawn brings you one day closer to that milestone.

be smaller; they often need to eat more frequently, and it may take more time for them to develop the ability to stay asleep for longer intervals.

Babies' sleep needs vary greatly. Some are able to stay asleep for five or six hours at a stretch as young as six weeks old. Others may take six months before they can sleep this long. There is no way to anticipate when that particular milestone will occur for each of your multiples; just rest assured that it will happen eventually.

Coping with the Lack of Sleep

So you've accepted the fact that having newborn multiples is going to be physically exhausting at times. There are some strategies that will help you survive the trying time until you can catch up on sleep.

From the very beginning, establish healthy sleep habits for your babies. The cozy, dark environment of the womb didn't distinguish between night and day, so newborns need some time to adjust to the new schedule. Many are born with their days and nights mixed up, being most alert in the middle of the night and sleeping soundly throughout the day. To encourage them to learn the difference, you can stimulate their senses when they are awake during the day, and keep things still and quiet at night. For example, use bright lights, background music, and a cheerful voice during daytime feedings, but keep the lights dim and your voice low at night.

Swaddling, the practice of wrapping babies "burrito style" in soft blankets, is comforting to many babies and may help them to feel snug and secure while sleeping. It's most commonly used with newborns who are still accustomed to the close confines of their mother's womb. Research has shown that swaddled babies sleep more deeply and fall back asleep more readily when awakened. It's also been proven to reduce the risk of sudden infant death syndrome (SIDS) because it keeps babies in the safest position, sleeping on their backs. Babies usually outgrow the comforting effects of swaddling after a month or two.

Some families find it helpful to take a tag-team approach in order to provide each parent with an opportunity for uninterrupted sleep. Mom might take the 9:00 p.m. to 2:00 a.m. shift, then Dad takes over until the morning. If you have access to helpers, whether hired or willing volunteers, make the most of their assistance while you catch up on rest.

Finally, make resting a priority. Napping can be restorative when you can't get a full night's sleep. Sleep when the babies sleep; don't try to use that time to catch up on other things. Housework can wait!

Mommy Must

Don't allow young infants to sleep through their feedings during the first week or so, especially if they were born early. They need consistent nutrition in order to grow and develop. It may seem like a blessing, but sleeping for more than five hours at a stretch during the first few weeks may actually be a sign of a weakened state or even dehydration.

Schedules to Save Your Sanity

Probably the most effective way to maximize your sleep opportunities is to get your babies on the same schedule. If you can feed them all at the same time, and get them to sleep at the same time, then you've won the game. Because every infant is an individual, that is not always possible, but it is reasonable to establish a schedule that works out most of the time.

Ideally, feeding on demand is the recommended approach for nurturing a singleton newborn. However, most parents of multiples find that it is more efficient to implement a more scheduled routine. That's not to say that you should ignore your babies' cues. You should never deny food to a hungry baby or ignore a baby's cries. Rather, you can gently encourage the babies to follow a complementary schedule by putting them to sleep together, changing diapers at the same time, and initiating simultaneous feedings.

Your schedule should be an organic plan that is constantly updated to meet your babies' changing needs, as well as the rest of the family's activities. You

Mommy Knows Best

Growth spurts are good! They usually come before a period of increased sleeping. They frequently occur at about two weeks, six weeks, three months, and six months, but babies' timetables vary greatly.

may encounter times when the babies appear to be hungrier more frequently. This behavior often precedes a growth spurt. During this enhanced period of growth and development, you'll need to adapt your schedule to meet their demand.

Easing your babies into a sleep routine will also help them to sleep longer and more soundly. Don't expect them to follow a sleep routine immediately, however. It will take some time to establish an acceptable routine, as the babies develop the ability to sleep for longer stretches at a time and concentrate their sleep hours overnight. But it's never too early to start constructing bedtime routines, using patterns of behavior that cue the babies that it's time to sleep.

Crying 101

Newborn babies are a feast for the senses: the sight of ten perfect tiny toes, the smell of their tender skin, the silky softness of their downy hair. One of the great joys of having multiples is being able to revel in these glorious sensations. However, the sound of multiple newborns is not always quite so pleasant for parents.

Mindful Mommy

Researchers estimate that babies spend one to two hours a day crying. Multiply that by two for twins or three for triplets, and that's an awful lot of bawling!

Newborn babies cry, and when you have multiples, it can sound like a never-ending cacophony.

Interpreting the Cries

Imagine if your babies were born with the ability to say, "Hi, Mom and Dad! We love our new home, but isn't it about time for dinner?" Unfortunately, language is an acquired skill, and until it develops, babies have to rely on other forms of communication.

Their primary mode is crying. If you think about crying as communication rather than as an annoying emission of useless sound, you'll be a much more effective—and much less frustrated—parent. It's your job to translate the cries and craft an appropriate response.

Babies cry for many reasons. They may be hungry and need to be fed. They may have a dirty diaper and need to be changed. They may be too warm or too cold. In addition to physical needs, they may also cry as a reaction to emotional needs, such as when they are over-stimulated, startled, or seeking the comforting touch of a loving parent.

As you get to know your newborns, you'll learn to interpret their cries more effectively. Simply spending

Mindful Mommy

With multiples, you'll face the additional challenge of distinguishing the individual cries of each baby. Even as newborns, your multiples are unique individuals. Each has his own needs and his own style of expressing them. It's important to respond to them as individuals, rather than always as a group.

time with each baby will help you understand their language of crying. Through trial and error you'll learn how to satisfy their needs. External cues may also be helpful in interpreting their cries. A baby who is crying because she is tired may yawn, while a hungry baby may gnaw on her fist. An unusually loud or high-pitched cry may indicate illness or pain.

Coping with Crying

Crying is a part of life when you're caring for babies. Unfortunately, it can often become a source of frustration. As a parent, you want so badly to be able to soothe and comfort your children, and inconsolable crying may feel like a failure of that goal.

When the crying becomes overwhelming, it's vital that you take steps to avoid losing control. There will be times when all the babies are crying at the same time, and you simply aren't able to stop it. When that happens, try one of these coping strategies:

- Walk away. Put the babies in a safe, secure place, such as a crib or playpen, and walk into another room for a minute. Take deep breaths to calm down. Count to twenty and then return to the babies.
- Use a calm, soothing voice to talk to the babies. It doesn't matter what you say. The sound of your voice may offer some temporary consolation, or at the very least, reassure them that you are aware of their needs.

- If their crying escalates over your calm voice, try singing! It may not stop the crying, but it will distract you from the chaos at hand and help you endure the maelstrom.

Above all, keep a sense of humor. In a few years, this will be a funny memory of life with multiples!

Details, Details, Details

With more than one baby in the house, it can be tough to keep track of all the details. Who ate what and when and how much? Was it Twin A who had a dirty diaper this morning or Twin B? Did you give all three babies their medicines or did someone get a double dose? Staying organized and having a system for record-keeping are important skills for new parents of multiples.

With your brain befuddled by lack of sleep, your first task is to remember which baby is which. If your multiples are identical, that can be tricky. Even dizygotic multiples can have remarkably similar appearances as newborns. The first step in keeping things straight is to make each baby easily identifiable at first glance. Some parents find it helpful to dress each multiple in a designated color. If color coordinating their wardrobe seems too complicated, consider other apparel clues: distinguishing hats, booties, or pacifier clips.

Many parents of monozygotic—or identical—twins worry that they won't be able to tell their twosome apart. Veteran parents, however, acknowledge that it's not as difficult as you would think. Even though identical twins have similar physical appearances, those that know them intimately will have no trouble distinguishing them. There are exceptions, of course. Everyone gets mixed up occasionally when they are bleary-eyed from lack of sleep!

Once you can easily identify each baby, you'll need an organized system of tracking their vital information. Many parents rely on a chart similar to that found in Appendix B. During the first weeks at home, it's vital to track crucial information about the babies' intake and output. If you are establishing breastfeeding, you'll want to keep track of how long each baby fed, and which breast they fed from. If you are combining breast milk and formula, a chart is very handy for keeping track of the alternating feedings. As gross as it sounds, monitoring the babies' diaper debris can help you ensure that they are getting proper nutrition and that their brand-new digestive systems are functioning properly.

Mindful Mommy

There's one downside to color-coding; eventually your babies will get undressed! If you rely too steadily on clothing cues, you'll likely become very confused when they're naked, for example, at bath time. Just in case, you can paint one tiny toe with a small dab of nail polish as a hint.

This is another instance where a chart or written record comes in very handy. Find a process that works for your family. You want a system that allows you to record important information without becoming cumbersome or an inconvenient burden.

Making Special Time for *Everyone*!

When you're a parent of multiples, you become very invested in ensuring that each child receives his or her "fair share." You expend a lot of energy trying to keep things equal. Many expectant parents of multiples express concern that they won't be able to bond equally with each child. Will they have enough love to go around? Fortunately, the reality of having multiples is that a parent's capacity to love only increases exponentially in proportion to the number of children. Multiples only multiply the amount of love in a family, they don't divide it!

What Is Bonding?

Modern parents put a lot of emphasis on the process of bonding with their babies. The term describes the intense attachment that forms between parent and child. In a nutshell, it's like falling in love with your baby. In the short term, it provides the motivation for parents to fulfill their child's needs, even at the sacrifice of their own. Over the long term, effective parent-child bonding is credited with numerous influences in a child's development. It provides the model for the child's future intimate relationships. It fosters a sense of security for the child and is said to enhance self-esteem.

Sometimes bonding occurs instantaneously after birth, but for other families, it develops over time with routine care giving. Sometimes the process is interrupted—for example, in situations where parents and child are separated shortly after birth, perhaps by a medical event. Such is frequently the case with multiples, many of whom are born prematurely or with other medical concerns. However, these impediments should not diminish bonding if parents are determined to overcome them.

Bonding with More Than One

There are many ways that parents of multiples can enhance their bond with their children. The strengthening of the emotional connection between parent and infant is accomplished by touch and smell. As much as circumstances permit, spend time holding and cuddling each baby individually. Face-to-face interaction is also important; look into your babies' eyes at every opportunity.

Mommy Must

The process of bonding with babies was first defined in the 1970s by two professors of pediatrics, Dr. Marshall Klaus and Dr. John Kennell. Their research changed the way that hospitals handle babies immediately following birth, encouraging them to give mothers and babies time together to bond.

Any of the following activities may be helpful in enhancing bonding. Take turns with each baby.

- Infant massage or other loving touch
- Singing
- Reading (it's never too early to start!)
- Skin-to-skin contact
- Rocking
- Talking and playing

It's not uncommon for parents to occasionally feel more attached to one baby. There's nothing wrong with that, as long as the feelings of attachment do not cause you to neglect the other multiple(s). Most parents find that feelings of partiality alternate among the children over time. If you are feeling an enduring preference for one multiple, you can overcome it by consciously spending more time with the other baby or babies.

Out and About and *Okay*

Once you've mastered the routines at home, it's time to venture out into the world. You can't stay in the house forever! Getting out and about with infant multiples can be quite a challenge, requiring the planning skills of an army general, the packing power of a mule, and the arms of an octopus. There's no need to become a hermit, however. Some simple strategies will make on-the-go maneuvering more manageable.

The first requirement for heading out is a good stroller. You'll find that your investment in a quality double, triple, or quadruple stroller pays off the first time you leave the house. With newborns, you may need to adapt the stroller to accommodate their "floppy" bodies. If your model adjusts, fold down the seats to form an open carriage and lay the babies in the space. Or prop up the babies in their seats using rolled-up blankets or head rests to support their necks. (Chapter 8 includes lots of information to help you choose the right stroller.)

If you're traveling by car, it's imperative that your vehicle is equipped with approved infant car seats—one for each baby. In most states, the law requires that infants under twenty pounds be seated in the back seat in a rear-facing seat. Be sure that your car seats are properly installed. The make and model of your vehicle will determine the best arrangement of the seats within the car. Some cars are not wide enough to accommodate three seats across, so if you have triplets, or twins and an older child, you may have to consider other options and invest in a new vehicle.

Mommy Must

Before you head out for the first time, confirm your plans with your babies' doctor. Don't risk exposure to germs if your babies are still recovering from prematurity or are especially susceptible to illness, and stay home if the weather is particularly nasty.

Carrying Case: The Diaper Bag

A diaper bag is a standard accompaniment for any family on the go with a baby, but what if you have multiples? You'll want to stock your bag with plenty of supplies, but you don't necessarily need to double or triple up. You will need a larger bag, however. Alternative bag styles might be a better option when you have twins or more. Consider a backpack or a larger tote.

In addition to diaper supplies, carry an extra outfit for each baby and feeding supplies (if you'll be out during mealtime). If your babies are partial to pacifiers, make sure you stash extras, and that you have enough to go around. A portable pad or blanket is a handy addition as well, providing a sanitary spot for changes when facilities aren't available on the go. Bibs, burp rags, plastic bags, and antibacterial hand sanitizer will be very helpful for cleanups. You don't want your bag to become burdensome to carry, but other handy items you might include are: bottled water, toys (rattles, teething rings, or small books), medications, and an extra shirt for mom, just in case.

You may find it easier to have help the first few times you venture out. Often the first outing is to the

Mommy Must

Always keep your diaper bag packed and ready to go. Restock items that you've depleted as soon as you return home, so that you don't have to rush around the next time you're trying to get out the door.

143

pediatrician for a checkup, which can be a stressful experience in itself. You'll appreciate having an extra pair of hands available until you're comfortable juggling all the babies and their supplies on your own.

Handling Special Situations

Every set of multiples joins a unique family, with its own special routines, challenges, and relationship dynamics. Sometimes special family circumstances present extra factors to consider as you prepare for the arrival of your multiples. No matter how your family is set up, adding multiples will mean a great deal of additional joy and love.

If You're a Single Parent . . .

If you are facing multiple pregnancy and parenthood without a partner, you are likely all too aware of the additional challenges that lie ahead. You will be outnumbered, with more babies than adults in the household. You're going to need extra help, during pregnancy and beyond. It's never too early to start making arrangements for assistance. As your pregnancy progresses, a loss of mobility and a lack of energy may keep you from being productive.

However, the period of time when you will most require help is during your babies' infancy. With only two hands, it will be quite a challenge to manage the care of multiple newborns. You may want to consider live-in help for a few weeks or months. If you can afford it, hire a nanny or night nurse to provide assistance. As the months pass and you become adept at single-handedly caring for your multiples, you will likely find that your need for help decreases.

In parenting, a partner provides emotional as well as physical support. Joining a support group where you can share advice and companionship with other single parents can fill that role for you.

Adopting Multiples

There are many routes by which a family adopts multiples. It could be an international adoption, where you open your home to encompass needy children from another part of the world. Or maybe you became the legal parents of additional children due to circumstances that left their biological parents unable to care for them.

No matter how it came to pass, this unique and special way of forging a family has its own set of challenges and obstacles to overcome. For parents in this situation, the need for support is great. It's important to seek out resources that address the special concerns of adoptive parents, as well as those aimed at parents of multiples.

Mommy Must

Most mothers require some sort of help during labor and delivery. If the father of your babies is unable or unwilling to provide support, ask a relative or trusted friend to assume the role of labor coach. You can also hire a doula as a source of support.

Sometimes adoptive parents perceive a lack of acceptance from fellow parents of multiples, and identify more closely with other adoptive families. Fortunately, both types of support are accessible in most locales. Your local parents of multiples organizations may include members who have adopted multiples. In addition, organizations for adoptive parents provide support throughout the adoption process. Networking with these other parents who have similar experiences can be very valuable.

Multiple Multiples

A very few families are lucky enough to be blessed with multiple multiples: more than one set of twins, triplets, or more. It's hard to believe that some families could hit the jackpot more than once, but it does happen. With the increase in multiple birth mostly attributed to assisted reproduction, the trend in multiple multiples hasn't experienced the same drastic uprising. Often couples who have multiples after a complicated process of conception assistance don't go through the process more than once.

But in families that have a natural tendency toward twinning, it's not surprising. The factors

Mindful Mommy

There are more than 900 adoption-related support groups in North America. These groups give parents the opportunity to share their experiences and emotions, as well as information.

that influence multiple birth—hyperovulation due to advanced maternal age, fertility drugs, or genetic predisposition—remain elevated with subsequent pregnancies. If you have an increased likelihood of conceiving twins once, your chances are good that it will happen again.

However, those identified factors only apply to dizygotic (fraternal) twinning. If your existing multiples are monozygotic (identical), then your chances should be the same as anyone else's that your next pregnancy will be multiples, right?

Except that there are two aspects of having multiples to consider: your chance of conceiving multiples and your chance of sustaining a multiple pregnancy. The first of these refers to the process of multiple sperm meeting the multiple eggs, or the chance of a fertilized egg splitting. The second concerns the ability of the fertilized egg(s) to travel to the uterus, implant, and begin to develop.

Some theories hold that having a previous twin or multiple pregnancy increases the odds of having a subsequent one based on the second factor: the mother's ability to sustain the pregnancy. The reasoning is based on the high number of twin conceptions

Mindful Mommy

Experts claim that a previous twin pregnancy quadruples a woman's risk of having them again. That is, a woman who has already had twins is four times as likely to have them again as a woman who has only given birth to singletons, or has never had children at all.

that never result in the live birth of two babies. Early ultrasound has allowed the detection of multiple embryos within a few days after conception. However, it is estimated that only 20 percent of those early pregnancies produce two or more live babies nine months later.

Because the body may consider a multiple pregnancy to be an abnormality, it may reject the pregnancy, resulting in miscarriage (a total loss of the pregnancy) or vanishing twin syndrome (reabsorption of one or more of the embryos, leaving one healthy, surviving fetus). However, if the multiple pregnancy does persevere, the body accepts it as a normal state, and subsequent twin pregnancies are more likely to thrive.

Whether that theory holds true or not, there have been cases where families produced an incredible assortment of multiples. A Russian woman in the eighteenth century reportedly gave birth to an astonishing amount: four sets of quadruplets, seven sets of triplets, and sixteen sets of twins. Several families have had twins followed by higher order multiples. In 2002 a set of quintuplets were born to a Pennsylvania

Mommy Knows Best

The popular children's book series *The Bobbsey Twins* featured a family with two sets of fraternal twins. Nan and Bert were about four years older than their younger twin siblings, Flossie and Freddie, when the series began, but in subsequent books their ages ranged from six to twelve. This book can be helpful for both you and your children!

family with five-year-old twin boys. Most common, however, are double sets of twins within a family. About one in three thousand women give birth to two sets of twins. Meanwhile, one in 500,000 will have three sets.

For families having multiples again, the news can be a mixed blessing. On the one hand, you are all too aware of the hardships, and with other children to care for, you may not look forward to a complicated pregnancy or the added chaos of infant multiples. Yet you've been through the experience before—you know what to expect, and many of your worries and concerns can be set aside. As an experienced parent, you've mastered the basics of baby care, and have developed efficient routines and shortcuts. You're an old pro, and can look forward to the additional joy that more multiples will bring to your unique family.

Caring for Premature Multiples

When babies are born too early, many of their body's organs and systems are immature, unable to function properly on their own. Fortunately, medical science has the ability to help those babies stay alive until they can sustain themselves. While it's not the ideal way to begin life, these babies are remarkably adaptive and can usually overcome their early start after a few weeks in the hospital.

Premature babies will be cared for in a NICU (Neonatal Intensive Care Unit). Having one child in the hospital is stressful, but having two, three, or even more critically ill preemies can push parents to the edge. Sometimes during the NICU experience, it may seem that every improvement is accompanied by one or more additional problems. Because your premature babies have missed out on crucial development time in the womb, they are being forced to adjust to life in a harsher environment, and the impact of that is manifested in many different ways. Oftentimes, the very treatments that are intended to preserve their life cause damage and further complications.

Preemie babies face a daunting array of challenges. Nearly every physical system is affected. Some of the issues can be addressed medically, with drugs, treatments, and even surgery. Others simply require the passage of time and will resolve with maturation.

The consequences of premature birth vary from short-term to long-lasting. Some are major disabilities while others are minor inconveniences. How prematurity will affect your babies depends a great deal on how early they were born. One of the most difficult aspects of having premature babies is not knowing where they will land within the spectrum of severity.

Once your babies have stabilized and conquered some of their more acute medical challenges, their main requirement will be time to grow and develop. Usually babies remain hospitalized until the time of their original due date, so it could be many weeks or months until they are big enough and strong enough to go home with you.

Most NICU hospitals have a support network for parents of preemies, and many of the members will be fellow parents of multiples. Talking to other parents who have experienced the NICU can be very reassuring. You'll realize you are not alone in your journey and that other babies have survived more severe challenges than yours.

Loss of a Multiple

Unfortunately, the complications that besiege multiple pregnancies sometimes result in the loss of one or more babies. Miscarriage, stillbirth, intrauterine fetal death, prematurity, and SIDS are all more common in multiples than in singletons. In addition, monozygotic multiples face potentially fatal complications such as twin-to-twin transfusion syndrome and conjoined twinning. No matter when a loss occurs, whether in the first trimester or after birth, it presents a complex situation for parents and any surviving multiples.

Mindful Mommy

About twenty years ago, babies born prior to twenty-eight weeks gestation were not considered viable. However, advances in medical technology now make it possible for some infants as young as twenty-three weeks to survive.

Parents dealing with the loss of one or more multiples may follow an atypical pace and pattern of grief. When there are surviving multiples, they are told to focus on their living children and to consider themselves lucky that there are survivors. They'll experience a wide range of emotions, including anger toward other families with multiples or guilt about their inability to prevent their child's death. They may be extremely overprotective of their surviving child(ren) or, conversely, emotionally disconnected because the remaining multiple(s) are a constant reminder of the loss. They may try to deny the loss by focusing intently on the survivor(s). Or they may feel intensely determined to keep alive the memory of the lost babies, to the exclusion of other children.

CLIMB, the Center for Loss in Multiple Birth, recommends some strategies for parents of multiples trying to cope with the loss of one or all of their babies. First, they urge parents to take the opportunity to hold and spend time with each baby, even while dying or after death. Often in the crisis of a medical situation, parents of multiples are denied a peaceful opportunity to say goodbye to their child.

Mindful Mommy

Losing a multiple is a unique kind of bereavement. Parents may not deal with the loss in the same way as parents mourning for a singleton. In addition to losing a precious child, they may also grieve the loss of the multiples' identity, as "the twins" or "the triplets."

This special time may take place at the hospital or later, at the funeral home. They also encourage parents to record the events of their lost child's life, no matter how brief, by taking pictures or videos, and by collecting mementos, such as a footprint, lock of hair, hospital bracelet, or blanket.

As part of the grieving process, many parents find it helpful to obtain a medical conclusion as to what went wrong. An autopsy or pregnancy loss evaluation can provide answers that alleviate the parents' sense of guilt or blame, as well as assist them in making decisions regarding future pregnancy care.

Grief counseling is highly recommended for parents who experience the loss of a multiple. Your hospital may be able to suggest a local resource, or CLIMB can put you in touch with counselors or support groups in your area. Often, delayed feelings of grief or depression surface on significant dates, such as birthdays or anniversaries, and parents continue to need support for years after the loss.

If there are surviving multiples, you will likely be very concerned with helping these children cope with the loss of their co-twin or co-multiple. It can be

Mommy Knows Best

Many parents who experience a loss find it comforting to send out a special announcement that explains the birth and death of their multiple(s). Samples of this type of correspondence can be found at CLIMB's Web site, *www.climb-support.org*.

a difficult parenting challenge. It's important to be honest with children about their origin in life. Even if young children don't seem to recall the presence of a twin or co-multiple, some research indicates that a subconscious awareness does exist. These children may grow up with a sense of something missing in their lives. They may experience survivor guilt, wondering why they survived when their sibling did not. The Twinless Twins International Support Group, established by a man who lost his twin brother in an accident, can provide support to children in this situation as well as to their parents.

Chapter 8

Multiple Choices

DECISIONS, DECISIONS, DECISIONS . . . As a parent of twins or multiples, you'll face many important choices about how to care for and raise your children. How will you feed your babies? Where will they sleep? What will you call them? Many of these choices will have to be determined even before your babies arrive, so it's never too early to start thinking about your options.

Breastfeeding or Bottle-feeding?

As soon as your babies are born, you'll be faced with a tough parenting choice: how to fill their hungry tummies. Instinct and scientific research confirm that breastfeeding is best, yet formula marketers offer assurance that their products offer healthy convenience. With more mouths to feed, efficiency is a priority but not at the expense of the babies' health and well-being. Ultimately, there is no right or wrong choice, only what works best for your family.

Making the Decision

To make an informed decision about feeding your multiples, it's important to understand the advantages and disadvantages of each method. No matter what you choose, you are likely to encounter opposition about your choice. Breastfeeding advocates will try to make you think you're sacrificing your babies' well-being if you give them bottles. At the other extreme, your friends and even some medical professionals may call you crazy and try to dissuade you from exclusively breastfeeding them. Ultimately, you have to do what's best for your family; that may be breast-feeding, bottle-feeding, or a combination of both.

Take the opportunity during pregnancy to research the issue. Books, magazines, and Web sites will all reveal useful factual information. Fellow parents of multiples are another valuable resource.

Whatever you decide, allow yourself the freedom to change your mind. You simply have no way of knowing what the future holds. Ruling out one option or the other may create more difficult circumstances for you in the long run. Even the most experienced breastfeeding advocate may find it overwhelming to nurse triplets, while the most reticent

Mommy Knows Best

As you talk to other mothers about their experience, ask them how they arrived at their choice and why it worked best for them. Pay particular attention to circumstances that closely resemble your own—for example, previous nursing experience (or lack of it), working or stay-at-home parents, or supertwins.

may feel compelled to nurse if her premature twins would benefit from breast milk.

Breastfeeding Multiples

The numerous benefits of breastfeeding are undeniable. For multiples, who are often at a developmental disadvantage due to low birth weight or prematurity, being breastfed can give them a wonderful boost. Consider the following benefits:

- Nursing aids in the development of the jaw, teeth and face.
- Breast milk protects infants from illness, infection, and allergies.
- Studies have shown that breastfed babies have higher IQs.
- Breastfed babies grow up to have fewer incidences of obesity and hypertension.
- The close contact between mother and babies while nursing enhances bonding and helps the babies feel secure.

Breastfeeding also benefits you in several ways. For example:

- Nursing after childbirth stimulates the uterus to return to normal more quickly.
- Mothers who breastfeed generally lose weight more rapidly.
- Some evidence suggests that breastfeeding reduces the mother's risks of certain cancers.

- It's readily available; you won't have to spend time mixing or reheating bottles.
- It's free!

Breastfeeding Twins

Since most mothers have two breasts, it is often convenient to nurse both babies simultaneously. It saves a great deal of time, but can be tricky at first. For infant twins, the football hold works well, especially for mothers who have delivered via cesarean section. This position keeps the bulk of the babies away from the tender incision site. As the twins get bigger, the parallel or "spoons" hold is convenient, while the criss-cross and front-V positions are ideal for older babies who don't require as much head support. A good supply of pillows will support the babies so that you can keep your hands free.

Breastfeeding Triplets or More

Most mothers of higher order multiples find it easier to use a rotation feeding schedule. For example, Babies A and B will nurse at the breast while Baby C receives a bottle of expressed breast milk. At the next feeding, Babies B and C are breastfed and

Mindful Mommy

Breastfeeding works on a supply and demand system. The more you breastfeed, the more milk your body will produce. Nursing often and allowing the babies to empty both breasts will help you establish an ample supply of milk.

1. Football hold

2. Parallel hold

3. Criss-cross hold

4. Front-V hold

Baby A receives a bottle. At the third feeding, Babies A and C are at the breast while Baby B takes the bottle. Another approach is tandem breastfeeding, or feeding each baby one after the other. It requires a lot of time and patience but allows each baby to have individual time with mom and ensures ample milk production.

Taking Care of Mom

If you're trying to produce milk for two or more babies, you'll have to eat enough to compensate. Experts recommend adding about 500 extra calories to your normal pre-pregnancy diet, approximately the amount found in a peanut butter sandwich or a cup of ice cream, but that's just for one baby! You'll have to adjust accordingly depending on how many babies you're feeding. Of course, that doesn't mean you should eat two cups of ice cream. What food you eat has a big impact on the quality of the breast milk that you produce. Choose foods with nutritional power, not the empty calories of junk food.

In addition to eating enough, you've also got to drink! It's much easier for your body to make milk if it's fueled with lots of liquids. Water is always the best choice, but juices and milk are good options also.

For moms of preemies or higher order multiples, pumping breast milk is a necessity; even mothers of full-term twins will find it to be a benefit. While a hand pump is useful for initial expressing of milk to establish supply, rent or buy one of the more powerful electric pumps for collecting milk in great quantities. A product with double suction cups will allow you to pump both breasts simultaneously. It's a tremendous timesaver and regulates milk production equally on both sides so that you don't end up lopsided!

Mommy Must

Breast milk should be refrigerated unless it is going to be used immediately. Refrigerated milk should be consumed within a week, but it will keep in the freezer for months.

Bottle-Feeding

There are many reasons why families with multiples elect to bottle-feed their babies. It definitely offers several advantages over breastfeeding, most notably that it allows someone other than you to be the primary source of food! Modern infant formulas, while not as perfectly nutritionally sound as breast milk, provide a healthy alternative with the convenience of bottle delivery.

Many bottle-feeding systems are available, and all have their own unique features. Ultimately, the best product is the one that works best for you and your babies. Younger infants need smaller four- or six-ounce bottles with low-flow nipple holes. As the babies grow, however, a feeding may average more than eight ounces, requiring larger bottles and nipples that allow a faster delivery of formula. You'll need at least one bottle per baby, but it's much more convenient to have a surplus.

Proper positioning of the babies for feeding is important. Be sure to support the babies' heads and bodies securely. You can bottle-feed both babies simultaneously if it is convenient. Refer to the diagrams for nursing positions earlier in this chapter

Mindful Mommy

Bottle-feeding requires a stockpile of supplies, and when there's more than one baby, all of the bottles, nipples, and formula may fill an entire pantry! It's always good to keep plenty on hand—running out when you have two or more hungry infants is not an option.

and emulate them for bottle-feeding; the close contact and intimacy is important for bonding. As with nursing, you'll enhance the babies' visual and cognitive development if you feed on alternate sides at each feeding.

Combination Approach

Some families find that a combination of breast and bottle works best for feeding their babies, as this offers the advantages of both methods. Alternating between nursing and giving a bottle of either formula or expressed breast milk allows fathers and helpers an opportunity to feed a baby and gives mom a much-needed break. There are several ways to combine approaches.

Alternate babies: One gets the breast, the other gets the bottle, and they switch at the next feeding.

Alternate feedings: Breastfeed all babies one time, bottle-feed the next.

Day/night rotation: Breastfeed during the day, bottle-feed at night. Alternately, working moms

Mindful Mommy

Although it's tempting, and sometimes a matter of necessity, bottle propping is discouraged. Instead, consider a hands-free bottle, like the Podee products, for those times when you have more babies than hands.

who are away from home during the day would utilize the opposite approach.

As needed: Primarily breastfeed, but supplement with a bottle when mom needs a break.

The Diaper Dilemma

The daunting task of diapering your babies is likely to be one of the most significant challenges you'll face as a parent of multiples. The good news is that it's only a temporary responsibility; eventually your kids will grow up and learn to use the bathroom. In the meantime, your goal is to devise an effective diaper system that makes the chore tolerable for everyone involved.

Your first challenge is to confront the ultimate diaper dilemma: cloth or disposable? If you've already made this decision for previous children, there's no real reason to change your habits for multiples. Whatever satisfies your personal cost, conscience, and convenience qualifications is the right choice. For first-timers, here's an overview of the advantages and disadvantages of each option.

Disposable diapers offer the benefit of convenience. They are ready to use, easy to put on and take off, and require the diaperer to have minimal contact with the offensive contents. Used disposables go out with the trash and can easily be discarded when you're out and about. Absorbent materials mean that babies' bottoms may stay drier, cleaner, and more comfortable. The downside is that these diapers are costly (for both consumers and the environment). Even when bought in bulk at a discount, each diaper change can take about fifteen cents out of your pocket. When you tally the total over your babies' diaper lifetime, the cost easily reaches into the thousands of dollars.

Cloth diapers have their associated costs as well; namely, the water consumed to wash them. Unless you're willing to use organic cotton products and wash all the diapers yourself, your efforts have a negligible impact on the problem. The products and treatments used by professional diaper services arguably have just as many negative environmental consequences as disposable diapers. Likewise, a family's cost to use a diaper delivery and cleaning service rivals the price of disposables.

Cloth diapers do have several qualities to recommend them. New styles function much like disposables; the days of pinning bunches of cloth are long gone, and comfortable covers are available in a wide range of colors and fashions. The natural fabric of cloth may be more comfortable for babies with skin allergies or sensitivities, and may reduce occurrences of diaper rash in all babies.

You'll need diapers on the go as well as at home. A well-stocked diaper bag will be your lifeline for managing your multiples out in the world. Keep it stocked with eight to ten diapers, a travel case of wipes, antibacterial hand cleaner, one change of clothes per baby, a blanket or pad, burp rags, and sealable plastic bags for disposing of dirty diapers.

Crib Notes

One of the biggest decisions parents of multiples will make about their babies concerns sleeping arrangements. Cribs are a big-ticket item in the nursery; not only do they consume a lot of floor space in a room, but they can also consume a big chunk of the budget!

Initially you won't necessarily need an individual crib for every baby. Two or even three infants can easily share a sleeping space during the first few months. Instead of a crib, you may prefer to keep the babies close at hand by having them sleep with you, or nearby in a bassinet, cradle, portable crib, or Moses basket. Eventually, however, you'll want to provide a designated, segregated spot for each baby in order to ensure secure and uninterrupted sleep for everybody. Once the babies are old enough to roll or scoot around, they can disturb each other, and that's the time to invest in additional cribs.

Mommy Must

When choosing cribs for your babies, follow established safety guidelines, such as those developed by the U.S. Consumer Product Safety Commission. You'll find up-to-date safety information at their Web site, *www.cpsc .gov/index.html*.

Another factor to consider when choosing cribs is longevity. Many families find it convenient to keep twins or more sleeping in cribs much longer than they would a singleton, perhaps even up to the age of three. In that case, the multiples may move right into—pardon the pun—twin beds. However, if you anticipate the need for an intermediate sleeping arrangement, toddler beds, with their protective railings and smaller mattresses, may be a viable option. Some crib models convert to toddler beds, extending their usefulness.

Cribs and baby bedding can be expensive, with fancy solid wood items retailing for well over $1,000. When you're faced with buying two or more at the same time, it may make sense to investigate secondhand products. Local mothers of multiples clubs are a wonderful source for locating secondhand sets of cribs, as well as other baby equipment. When purchasing used products, be sure that they are in good condition and meet established safety guidelines.

Stroller Style

The stroller is perhaps the most crucial piece of equipment you will buy as a parent of multiples. Unless you plan to remain confined to your home until your children can walk themselves to school, you will need a good stroller to maneuver them through the world. Many families find that their stroller remains a convenient and safe method of transportation for several years, so it is worth investing in a quality product that will withstand some wear and tear. Think of it as a vehicle for your babies and give your purchase as much consideration as you would if you were buying a family car.

The Great Debate

Ask any parent of twins about their stroller, and they'll likely give you a passionate response as to why their model is the best choice available. However, there is no one perfect stroller; if there was, everyone would own it! Your perfect stroller is the one that meets your family's needs. There are two basic styles of strollers. Each style has advantages and disadvantages and parents are pretty evenly split in their preferences.

Tandem Strollers

Tandem strollers have seats arranged in a straight line, with one behind the other. The seats may both face forward or face each other. They're more readily available because they aren't used exclusively for twins. Many models are actually designed for two singleton siblings.

Tandems are generally longer and more slender than side-by-side models and some people find them easier to maneuver through narrow spaces, such as shopping center aisles and doorways. Some offer the convenience of a travel system that functions in combination with infant carrier/car seats.

Side-by-Side Strollers

Side-by-side strollers are a more traditional type of twin stroller. They operate most efficiently with two children of equal weight, and provide adequate leg and head room for both as they grow. One distinct advantage is that both children are positioned with an equal viewpoint, which is the arrangement most twins seem to prefer.

Side-by-sides are wider than tandems but have a shallower profile. That gives the stroller pusher more control and puts the babies in a closer arm's reach. Some models of double jogging strollers offer durable details perfect for outdoor use. Unfortunately, many parents find their width hard to deal with in crowded or constricted locations.

Strollers for Triplets or More

Stroller options for higher order multiples are more limited, and more costly. You'll have to carefully evaluate how you'll utilize the equipment and anticipate whether the investment is worthwhile. You may wish to consider a combination of single and double strollers, or investigate the availability of a secondhand stroller.

Mindful Mommy

One potential pitfall of side-by-side models: They put your twins in full view for the whole world to see. There is no chance of being anonymous! If you think that being the center of attention will bother you, minimize it by sticking with a tandem-style stroller. They are more efficient at keeping the babies out of the public eye.

What's in a Name?

Selecting names for your children is one of the most long-lasting decisions you will make on their behalf. It can be a difficult decision, especially considering that you have yet to meet the little creatures to which you are assigning a lifelong label. With multiples, you not only have to consider the individual nomenclature, but you'll also want to think about how their names interact as a group.

Naming style is a source of controversy among the multiples community. Some families try to avoid names that rhyme, start with the same letter, or otherwise appear matched. They feel that it compromises their multiples' sense of individuality. Others enjoy choosing a corresponding combination that clearly indicates their children's status as multiples. Ultimately, it's a matter of personal preference. You will find, however, that there is an expectation that twins and multiples' names should be coordinated, and you may be met with a reaction of disappointment if you announce unrelated names.

To start the process, brainstorm a list of names that you and your partner like. You can turn to baby naming books and Web sites for ideas. If you know the sex of your babies, you can focus exclusively on names that match their gender. Have some backups for the opposite sex, though, just in case there is a surprise!

Once you have a list of possibilities, consider how the names work in combination. Even if you want to avoid matching names, you will probably want to select names with similar styles or a sense of balance; for example, names that are all very feminine, monosyllabic, or of comparable meaning. Keep in mind any potential nicknames for each choice.

Can't come up with anything? There's no rule that you have to choose names before the babies arrive. Brainstorming names can be a fun diversion during labor. Or, you may wait until you meet them to make a decision. Laying eyes on your precious newborns might provide the inspiration to make the perfect choice.

Dressing Your Duo

The issue of coordinated dressing is a hot topic among parents. Some find it a cute and fun aspect of having multiples. Others believe that it detracts from their children's individuality. No research exists to confirm that the practice is damaging to multiples' sense of self, but you should be sensitive to your children's feelings about the issue once they're old enough to express a preference. In the meantime, your babies

Mommy Knows Best

Deciding which baby receives which name can be a tricky determination. In utero, most multiples are identified by the labels "Baby A," "Baby B," "Baby C," and so on. You might select names that start with those letters. Other families assign names based on birth order. The first baby to be delivered receives one name, and the second another.

won't care as long as their clothes are comfortable and cozy, so take advantage of their infancy to dress them up to your heart's content.

If you're conflicted about the issue, consider a compromise. Save the matching outfits for photo opportunities or special occasions. Use coordinated or similar outfits, rather than exact matches, to experience the fun without creating a cookie-cutter effect. Or assign each multiple a color and then choose clothing (and later, toys, sippy cups, and everything else!) to match. Not only does it help to identify the individual child, but it makes it much easier to settle ownership disputes when they reach the age of such squabbles.

Choosing a Pediatrician

In addition to prenatal care for your pregnancy and delivery, you'll need to choose a caregiver for your multiples after they're born. If you have older children, you may already have a pediatrician or family practitioner. That individual can probably serve your needs for your new arrivals, as well. However, you

Mommy Knows Best

Duplicate outfits can be a curse or a convenience; it's certainly easier to tell twins apart when they're dressed differently. However, when you're overwhelmed with the day-to-day details of caring for twin infants, it's much simpler to choose one outfit rather than two.

may want to consider some of the unique needs of multiples.

If your babies are born prematurely or have special needs after birth, they will be treated in the hospital by a neonatologist, a specialist who treats infants with serious illness, injury, or birth defects. However, most newborns only require a pediatrician, a doctor who specializes in treating babies and children.

You'll want to interview and select a pediatrician during your pregnancy, so that he can visit the babies when they're born. If you do not designate a specific caregiver, your babies will be attended in the hospital by a doctor on call. Or, if your chosen pediatrician is not affiliated with the hospital where you deliver, you may be assigned to another doctor until they are released from the hospital.

While it is helpful to have a doctor that has previous experience with twins or multiples, it's not as crucial as during pregnancy. Now that your babies have arrived, they should be treated as individuals, and you'll want doctors that are qualified to handle their individual issues. However, there are some criteria to consider when choosing a doctor for your multiples. These are mostly issues of convenience, not qualifications, but they may weigh in your decision.

Location, Location, Location

Choose a doctor that practices in a location and setting that is easily accessible. You'll be paying plenty of visits to his office in the next few years; minimize the hassles as much as you can. When you visit the office, check out the facilities. Is it easy to park and enter the building? Can you easily negotiate the entry, doorways, and stairways or elevator with a stroller or with your hands full? Is the office staff friendly and helpful?

In addition, find out the practice's policies. What happens after hours? Do they offer telephone support, such as an Ask-A-Nurse service? What if your doctor is unavailable? Are their partners or nurses available that you can see as an alternative?

Cost

Some pediatricians will offer a discount on well-baby care for multiples, perhaps a percentage off the charge for the second, third, or fourth baby. It doesn't hurt to ask!

Philosophy

When you interview potential doctors, find out their stance on parenting issues that are important to you, such as breastfeeding, family bed, immunizations, and circumcision. Only a face-to-face interview will reveal whether you are compatible with a doctor. It's important that you feel comfortable with

Mommy Knows Best

Ask your fellow parents of twins or multiples for recommendations. They'll give a glowing endorsement of doctors that are good candidates, and you'll know to steer clear of any that generate complaints.

her personality, and that you trust her ability to care for your children. You should not feel intimidated or rushed when you ask questions. Finally, you should get a sense that the doctor respects your intuition as parents.

Chapter 9

Oh, Baby, Baby!

AFTER THE WHIRLWIND OF the first few weeks with newborns, life settles down somewhat. You're getting to know your babies, and learning your way through the puzzle of parenthood. You've figured out what works—and what doesn't—and have mastered many tricks for getting them to eat, sleep, and stop crying. While you're probably feeling a bit more confident about managing your multiples, there may still be days when you feel overwhelmed by the task of caring for them. It's normal! Recognize that having even one baby is a challenge, and give yourself credit for coping with two, three, or more.

Easing into a Routine

Many parents find it efficient, even necessary, to maintain some sort of schedule in caring for multiple babies. Parents who have had singleton babies previously often find that they adopt a much more structured approach when caring for twins or more. Every family is unique and each baby is an individual, so there is no master schedule that works for everyone. The trick is in finding what works best for you.

Routines at Home

As your babies grow, they will sleep for longer stretches and remain awake for longer periods of time. Their developing digestive systems are able to consume and process larger amounts of food to sustain them longer between feedings. Whether you're nursing, using bottles, or a combination of both, the daily routine will begin to evolve into a set of mealtimes rather than round-the-clock feeding. In between meals, your babies will nap, but will also enjoy longer periods of wakefulness, ideal times for playing, bonding, and practicing new skills. It can be a wonderfully exciting time, as your multiples discover the world around them, as well as each other.

It's also a time for you to catch your breath—and catch up on the things that have gone undone while you've juggled the demands of infants. You may find more opportunities in your days to tackle housework, check e-mail, or run errands. Just as you establish

Mommy Must

Your baby equipment will get a lot of use during this time. Bouncy seats, Exersaucers, swings, and play yards are all good options for keeping babies safe and contained—yet also entertained—when you need your hands free.

new routines for your babies, you may find it helpful to create routines for your own responsibilities. Use afternoon naptime to run a load of laundry or to mop the kitchen floor. Schedule some relaxation time just for you after they go down at night. Hire a teenager to accompany you on errands one afternoon a week.

Away from Home

If you're a stay-at-home mom, you'll be responsible for your babies' routine throughout the day. If you're returning to work after having twins or multiples, you'll have to partner with your caregiver to establish a schedule. As you work out the details, try to incorporate some consistency with your lifestyle in your off-time. It will ensure more peaceful transitions between work days and weekends and make things easier for babies, your caregivers, and yourself.

If you've been breastfeeding your babies, your routine will change when you return to work. You can maintain the benefits of breastfeeding by expressing and collecting milk for a caregiver to give the babies by bottle when you're away. Start a pumping routine a couple of weeks before you're due to start work in order to build up a supply of expressed milk.

To ensure a successful pumping session, follow these guidelines:

- Drink a glass of water before starting.
- Sit down in a comfortable, peaceful location.

- Look at your babies or a picture of your babies to encourage let-down of your milk.
- Use the proper collection receptacle for your breast pump model.
- Label the expressed milk and store it immediately after it is collected.

Evening Routines

Evenings can be a particularly chaotic and challenging time for families, and the chaos is often multiplied for families with multiples. There's a lot to accomplish in a few hours as the day winds to an end, and often all of the parties involved are fatigued and fussy after the demands of the day.

Keeping things simple will make everyone a lot happier, starting with dinnertime. Enjoying time together should be the focus of your dinner routine. Save the elaborate cooking sessions for a time when your multiples are older and more independent. Prepare easy but nutritious meals, and make it a priority to spend time together as a family. The babies can be a part of the meal, too. Set up their bouncy seats or high chairs at the dining table and let them participate in the family interaction.

Mindful Mommy

If you have older children, they can be extremely helpful during this time, by passing supplies and entertaining the babies. They will enjoy participating in the babies' care and you'll appreciate the extra set of hands, however small!

Bath time is another routine that's often reserved for evenings. Although babies don't necessarily need a bath every day, many families find that a soothing bath is a perfect way to conclude the day's event and set the stage for the transition to bedtime. Bathing multiple babies can be quite an escapade! When they're younger, it's easier to bathe them one at a time. But once they can sit up securely, you can put them in the tub together using specially secured baby bath seats.

Bedtime may be the most anticipated routine of the day! A bedtime routine can become one of your most cherished rituals as a parent, and the traditions you create with your multiples as babies can carry on for years to come. Establishing a consistent bedtime routine will ensure that everyone gets better sleep; if your babies are able to settle down to sleep, so will you! Use patterns of behavior that cue the babies that it's time to sleep. For example, an evening routine of a bath, followed by a feeding and snuggle time, can help babies recognize that it's bedtime as you put them into their cribs.

Bedtime routines can be a group affair or a time for individual bonding. Create a relaxing atmosphere

Mindful Mommy

Your multiples can share a room, or even a crib, as long as they don't disturb each other's sleep. Many twins share a room until they start school, and higher order multiples may share space with a same-sex sibling for many more years.

with low lights or soft music. Spend a few moments in calm interaction with each baby. Say prayers, sing a song, or express your love with a special saying. It's never too early to start reading with your children, even if your babies don't understand a word that you're saying! Your bedtime routine is unique to your family; make it a special, enjoyable way to end the day.

Scheduling Flexibility

Your daily routines should follow your family's personality. Develop a routine that suits your babies' temperaments, as well as your family's needs. Remember that your babies are individuals and while it's generally easier to keep everyone on the same pace, parents of multiples have to allow for some flexibility.

Be willing to adjust your routines and schedules to accommodate your growing babies. Teething, growth spurts, illnesses, and the mastering of new skills can wreak havoc with the most carefully laid plans, making babies wakeful when they should be sleeping, fussy when they should be playful, and ravenous at odd hours of the day or night. Acknowledge these bumps in the road and remember, "This TWO shall pass . . . " Things will get back on track in a few days, and if not, it's time for a few adjustments. Babies aren't a precise science. While most parents of twins or multiples do find that keeping their babies on the same feeding and sleep schedule is most efficient, there are always exceptions, and you're the only one who can determine the best approach for your family.

Mommies of Multiples Do:
- Create routines that fit their family's lifestyle.
- Follow a consistent pattern of mealtimes, naptimes, and wakeful playtimes.
- Establish routines that help them accomplish their household responsibilities.
- Keep their babies on the same schedule if it works for everyone.
- Allow their daily schedule to change as their babies grow.

Mommies of Multiples Don't:
- Become inflexible—babies aren't automatons and there will be plenty of days when they don't conform to a schedule.
- Become surprised if both their babies develop diverse sleeping and eating habits over time. They are individuals, after all, and may have different metabolisms.
- Try to follow someone else's schedule; many multiples are born early and their timetable may be different from full-term babies.

Making Mountains Out of Milestones

The first year of a baby's life is full of exciting firsts: first words, first tooth, first steps. The changes that take place from month to month are astonishing. One of the most interesting aspects of having twins or multiples is that parents get to experience these special moments in duplicate or triplicate, within a close span of time. Where parents of singletons can only compare their children's development through the lens of flashback and memory, parents of multiples have an instant, side-by-side view, like a split-screen video.

With multiples, however, it's important to keep milestones in perspective. First, remember that multiples are individuals—not clones. Don't expect them to meet milestones on the same timetable; there's no need for concern if their "firsts" are separated by several days, weeks, or even months. Instead, enjoy the opportunity to watch their unique development. It's never too early to practice the habit of avoiding comparisons. As they get older, they'll get enough of that from society; as their parent, it's your job to encourage them just to be themselves.

Many twins and multiples experience delays in development, particularly if they are born prematurely. If your multiples were born prior to thirty-six weeks, you may want to factor in their adjusted age

Mindful Mommy

MOST (Mothers of Supertwins), an organization for parents of higher order multiples, recommends that parents seek medical evaluation at regular intervals and consider taking advantage of early intervention programs if their multiples need extra assistance overcoming developmental delays.

when assessing milestones. For example, if they were born at thirty-two weeks (eight weeks premature) on April 7th, their adjusted age on June 30th would be four weeks:

$$Adjusted\ Age =$$
$$Chronological\ Age - \#\ of\ Weeks\ Premature$$

It would not be unusual to observe characteristics of a one-month-old infant rather than a three-month-old baby. Consult your pediatrician for clarification on what to expect for your individual babies' developmental milestones.

Mommies of Multiples Do:
- Recognize developmental milestones. Your pediatrician can advise you on what to expect, or consult baby care guides or Web sites for information.
- Factor in your babies' adjusted age if they were born prematurely and adjust your expectations accordingly.

Mommies of Multiples Don't:
- Compare babies. They are individuals and each child has his or her own timetable for development.
- Worry if their multiples lag behind singleton babies of the same age. Even extremely premature infants can overcome developmental delays over time.

Here are some common developmental milestones.

By four months, most babies:
- Babble, coo, smile, laugh, and squeal
- Are able to control their head and hold it upright while in a prone position
- Roll over
- Bat at objects and can grasp some objects

By six months, most babies:
- Vocalize single consonant sounds (dada, baba)
- Sit with support
- Transfer objects from hand to hand or hand to mouth
- Start the teething process

By nine months, most babies:
- Understand a few simple words (mama, no, bye-bye)
- Crawl, creep, or scoot
- Sit independently

Transitioning to Solid Food

From day one and for the rest of their lives, mothers are very concerned with what their children eat! Just when you get the hang of breastfeeding or bottles, your multiples will be ready to move on to a new eating routine. If they were born early, it is possible that they will not be ready for solid foods at the four-to-six month timeframe suggested by the American Academy of Pediatrics, so check with your medical caregiver. Don't base your decision to start solid foods on the calendar, but rather on your babies' readiness for this new phase of their lives. It is even conceivable that each of your babies will have different stages of readiness depending on their individual development.

Eating is a transition process during the first year of your babies' lives. Generally, breast milk or formula will remain their primary source of nutrition, while solid food is a supplement. The recommended first food for babies is usually an iron-fortified rice cereal mixed with breast milk or formula to a soupy consistency. For the first offering, it may be easier to work with one baby at a time. Or, if you prefer for both babies to share the experience, choose a time when your husband or partner is available to lend a helping hand. Offer the food on the tip of your finger, or with a soft plastic spoon. If the baby thrusts the food out of his mouth with his tongue, he may not be ready. Try again in a few weeks. But if she

Mommy Knows Best

Your babies don't have to have teeth before they start solid foods. However, look for signs that the teething process has started; their drool contains enzymes that help them break down food before they have the teeth to chew it.

swallows and seems to enjoy the food, you can start incorporating it into her diet.

Introduce new foods one at a time, waiting a week or so in between new additions to give babies time to get used to each new taste. Look for signs of intolerance to new foods, such as a rash, fussiness, gassiness, or runny nose. Food allergies aren't necessarily a genetic condition, so even identical (monozygotic) twins can have different reactions. After rice cereal, you can try other appropriate foods. Discuss your options with your pediatrician, but traditional suggestions include mashed ripe bananas or pears, applesauce, cooked and mashed sweet potato, or carrots and mashed avocado. It's simple and economical to prepare these foods yourself, but jarred baby foods are a convenient option also, especially for busy parents of multiples.

Add new foods gradually over the course of weeks or months, including sources of protein like ground or pureed cooked meat, yogurt, oatmeal, cooked, mashed rice, or 100 percent fruit juice. (Avoid berry or citrus juices.) Finger foods—soft foods that your babies can pick up and self-feed—can be introduced at about nine months of age, or according to your

Mindful Mommy

Watching your multiples experience new tastes and textures can be quite amusing! They may or may not share the same taste preferences; one twin may love sweet potatoes while the other craves peas.

pediatrician's recommendations. Suggested foods include thoroughly cooked soft pieces of pasta, pieces of soft cheese or vegetables like green beans or carrots cooked until soft.

Share the Fare and Address the Mess

Hygiene experts will likely be horrified, but most parents of multiples find it convenient to feed their babies from a shared dish and spoon. Unless your babies have an illness or medical conditions that would discourage the practice, do what is most efficient at mealtime. You'll definitely save time by feeding both babies at the same time!

Feeding multiple babies can be a messy affair. If your kitchen can't accommodate multiple highchairs, consider some alternatives. Younger babies can be fed in a bouncy seat or infant carrier seat. Older babies that sit upright securely can use seats that attach to a table if space is at a premium. Of course, never leave babies unattended while eating.

Mealtime is an incredibly educational process for your babies. They're exploring their senses; beyond just tasting the food, they experiment with feel and texture by squishing it in their fingers, test the theory of gravity by dropping it on the floor, and develop their artistic talents by smearing colorful concoctions on their tray (or on each other!). Playing with their food is part of the process of eating for babies, but it can make a multiple-size mess for parents of twins or more. Put a plastic sheet or an old vinyl tablecloth or shower curtain under highchairs to contain the spills and splatters. Bibs are essential for protecting baby clothing—who has time for multiple outfit changes? Or go naked. Even though it isn't proper etiquette, babies are welcome at the table without a shirt. It saves time and loads of laundry.

Mommies of Multiples Do:
- Watch for signs of readiness and consult with their pediatrician before offering solid foods—babies born prematurely may be ready later than full-term babies.
- Start with rice cereal mixed with breast milk or formula to a soupy consistency, and use your finger or a soft spoon to place the cereal in each baby's mouth.
- Have a helper handy the first time you offer the babies solid food.
- Add new foods gradually and one at a time so that you can monitor each baby's reaction.
- If convenient and efficient, alternate feeding both babies at the same time from the same spoon if convenient.

Mommy Knows Best
You may want to give your babies their own spoon to hold while you feed them. They can practice self-feeding, but it also serves as a distraction from grabbing your spoon midway to their mouths.

- Stock up on plenty of bibs and washcloths to keep the mess at bay.

Mommies of Multiples Don't:
- Get surprised if their babies spit out solid food the first time they try it.
- Mix cereal or solid foods into a liquid and give it to their babies in a bottle.
- Allow babies to share food if they have an illness.
- Wait until babies are screaming with hunger to start mealtime.

Becoming Mobile— Creeping and Crawling

As newborns, babies are fairly stationary, content to lie quietly in a crib or to be held in the loving arms of a caretaker. But after a few months, they begin to wiggle and writhe, to push up and roll over, and eventually to sit upright. Then things get really interesting for parents of twins or multiples! It's one thing to take care of babies that stay in one place. When

Mindful Mommy

Keep in mind that your multiples may have different approaches to mastering their mobility. There's no one right way to crawl; each of your babies will learn to move around in his own way and on her own time. If you're concerned, your medical caregiver can offer some guidance on your babies' progress.

they start moving around—generally in different directions!—it takes a lot of energy to keep up. Life takes on a new dimension once your multiples get mobile.

Most babies start the process of scooting or crawling between six and ten months of age. However, some multiples may start later, especially if they experience developmental delays due to prematurity. The process generally begins once babies can sit upright without support. Your babies may begin to balance on their hands and knees, and then rock back and forth to propel themselves forward. Other babies don't do a traditional crawl. They may scoot along on their bottoms, using an arm to push forward or creep along the floor like a soldier. Still others never crawl at all, skipping this intermediary step altogether and going straight to upright walking.

This learning time can be an interesting period. Just when you thought that you were settling into a routine, you may notice deviations in the babies' sleeping and eating habits. They might even seem fussy or cranky. Just remember that they have a lot going on in their little lives. While your babies are working on their motor skills, they may be preoccupied with their task. Be patient, and give them plenty of opportunity to practice their skills.

Up until now, you've had a great deal of control over your babies' environment, making it easy to keep them safe from harm. As they make a move toward independent mobility, they'll gain access to more potential dangers. It's time to increase your vigilance. This is a good time to identify and organize designated "safe spots" within you home; places where your babies can be contained and isolated from hazards and harm. You can create a safe space by blocking out a room with gates and lockable doors, or by using secure baby equipment like play pens or play yards. Designate a spot within all the major zones of your home; near the kitchen, bedrooms, and main living area. You'll rely on these safe zones often throughout the day, when you need a bathroom break, are trying to prepare a meal, or when you need to attend to one baby while keeping the other out of trouble.

Mommies of Multiples Do:

- Recognize that mobile multiples are more vulnerable to hazards in the home, and maintain a safe and secure environment.
- Give their babies plenty of playtime on the floor to practice their crawling skills.

Mommies of Multiples Don't:

- Underestimate their crawling babies' ability to scoot out of range, often in opposite directions.
- Worry if their babies' crawling skills don't conform to a "typical" timeframe—many multiples experience delays.
- Turn their back on a mobile multiple in an unsafe space.

Making the Most of Playtime

The playful interaction between mother and child is one of the most enjoyable aspects of motherhood, and mothers of multiples have the added joy of watching their babies play together. The baby talk and singsong chatter . . . patty cake and peekaboo game . . . rattles and squeaky toys . . . all elicit giggles and squeals of joy. The fun is only multiplied with multiple babies. But what seems like play is actually a vitally important component of babies' physical, emotional, and mental development. The benefits of playtime are numerous, but the opportunities for productive play can be limited for parents of multiples. Not only are they busier—and usually sleepier!—than parents of singletons, but they have at least twice as many babies to nurture and entertain.

Fortunately, one of the benefits of having multiples is that more babies means more fun. Multiples become playmates for each other at a very early age, absorbing some of the burden from mom and dad to provide constant entertainment.

As infants, your babies spent a great deal of their time sleeping and eating, but they were also develop-

Mommy Knows Best

That doesn't absolve parents from the responsibility of playing with their babies, though! It's important to create opportunities for playful interaction, both as a family and on an individual basis, throughout your children's lives.

ing fine motor skills and processing sensory experiences as you held them, fed them, and rocked them to sleep. Now that they are a bit older, you can create more interactive playtimes. Spread out a blanket or mat and create a safe, comfortable area on the floor for "tummy time."

In years past, most babies slept on their tummies. But now, parents are encouraged to put their babies to sleep on their backs in order to decrease the risk of SIDS (Sudden Infant Death Syndrome) and multiple babies spend much of the rest of their time lying in bouncy seats and car seats. It's important to create opportunities during babies' wakeful periods to spend time face down so that they can learn to push up, roll around, and, eventually, start to crawl. You can give your babies toys to look at or play with if they have the ability to grip them. Place them face to face; they'll enjoy looking at each other. Or for even more fun, lie down on the floor with them.

The fun and games really begin once your babies can sit up, either with or without assistance. Use developmental toys to stimulate your babies' senses: toys with bright colors and distinct geometric patterns to look at; items with varying textures to feel,

Mommy Must

Alternate the tummy time experience to focus more individual attention on each child. If tummy time makes your babies fussy, start with short sessions and gradually increase the amount of time they spend.

both with hands and mouths; toys that squeak, buzz, toot, or make animal sounds.

Boo-Boos, Bugs, and Well Baby Checkups

In an ideal world, all babies would be happy and healthy for the first year of their lives. Unfortunately, that's not the case, and most parents have to contend with some illness or infirmity. There will likely be minor things like colds and ear infections or accidents that cause bumps or bruises. Some multiples will have to deal with major medical issues, perhaps complications related to premature birth or the development of an infection like RSV (Respiratory Syncytial Virus). Even healthy babies have to visit the doctor regularly for checkups and immunizations, and a routine doctor visit with multiples can present some interesting logistical challenges.

Cold Cases

No family is a fortress, and even the most fortunate will have to confront routine childhood ailments like

Mindful Mommy

It's never too early to start reading to children. Heavy duty board books or textured cloth books provide visual stimulation. You don't have to read the text verbatim; just talk about what you see on the page. Take turns reading with each baby individually as well as to the group.

colds, upset tummies, and skin rashes. With multiple babies in the home, you can be sure that what comes around will go around; once one baby is sick, the rest are likely to follow. Having sick babies is no fun, but most illnesses are fairly short-lived and inconsequential, if inconvenient. Sometimes the symptoms seem horrifying; barking cough (croup), raised red rash all over the body (roseola), blisters on the hands and feet (hand, food and mouth disease), white spots on the tongue (thrush), or diaper-destroying diarrhea (rotavirus). These and other common conditions are usually not serious, but you should always consult your doctor when one of your babies is sick.

Mommies of Multiples Do:

- Watch for common cold symptoms, like nasal discharge, low-grade fever, watery eyes, sneezing or coughing, and consult a doctor if their multiples are under three months old or particularly susceptible to respiratory infection.
- Wash their hands as often as possible to avoid spreading the virus from baby to baby.
- Try to keep things separate among the babies when one of your babies is sick, even though

Mindful Mommy

Even the healthiest babies are likely to have six colds before their first birthdays. Because the cold virus spreads so easily from person to person, your multiples can generously share their colds, back and forth throughout the season.

it's inconvenient. Use separate wash cloths, towels, and blankets.

- Offer plenty of fluids to keep babies hydrated.
- Avoid confined public places where germs can easily be spread by close contact.

Mommies of Multiples Don't:

- Let the babies share pacifiers, toys, feeding accessories (or anything else that is likely to go in their mouths) when they are under the weather.
- Expose their babies to cigarette smoke.

Visiting the Doctor

Since most doctors don't do house calls, you're going to have to make a trip to the office with your twins or multiples. Whether you're visiting for a routine checkup, an illness, or a minor emergency, it can be a harrowing experience. Sometimes just getting from the parking lot to the waiting room can be logistically intimidating! Then there is a series of waiting games, culminating in a rushed appearance with the doctor where you juggle cranky and uncooperative babies and try to answer questions and remember instructions without getting too frazzled.

Hopefully you've been able to establish a relationship with a medical caregiver that is accommodating to parents of multiples. A bit of preparation before a doctor visit will also help things go more smoothly. If possible, bring along a helper, an extra pair of hands

to help dress and undress babies, provide comfort, and keep the kids occupied so you can focus on your conversation with the nurse or doctor. It will also free up your hands so that you can write things down, the best cure for the mental mind-melt that tends to plague mothers of multiples.

Before you go, make a list of your questions and concerns, so that you're sure to cover everything while you're with the doctor. Pack a diaper bag with extra care, including extra clothes, diaper supplies, snacks, and entertainment. If your babies will be receiving immunizations, ease the pain with comfort items like a favorite blanket or pacifier, as well as a bit of baby acetaminophen if your doctor approves it.

Ongoing Medical Care

Some multiples will require ongoing medical treatment or therapy due to the effects of prematurity. Some may be administered at home, like breathing treatments, feeding tubes, or apnea monitors, while others will require a trip to the doctor's office.

In addition to routine checkups with your pediatrician, you may need to visit specialists to monitor your babies' development, including assessment of their vision, hearing, and motor skill development.

Having healthy multiples is challenging enough, and facing medical issues only increases the strain on parents. Here are some tips for parents who find themselves coping with medical complications (see the following page).

Mommies of Multiples Do:

- Find support by establishing a network of people that can offer physical and emotional help.
- Learn CPR so that they're prepared in the event of an emergency.
- Educate themselves fully about each child's condition and keep individual records.

Mommies of Multiples Don't:

- Let themselves get rundown. Taking care of themselves makes them a better mother to their children.

Chapter 10

Approaching Toddlerhood

LIFE WITH OLDER BABIES is a daily series of explorations and discoveries. Your babies are becoming toddlers who can communicate with you (and each other), transport themselves from place to place, and get into anything—and everything. But it's also a fascinating time for parents of twins and multiples, who have the privilege of watching their babies turn into little people with individual personalities, and an amazing relationship with each other.

Up(right) and Away

They've gone from scooting to crawling to cruising, and now they're walking. Twins on two legs are a force to be reckoned with, and life is going to take on a decidedly different pace. On one hand, having walkers takes a load off of your back and frees up your arms since you don't have to carry your babies everywhere they go. However, multiples on the move have their own ideas about where and when they're going to go, and there will be times when you feel like a shepherd trying to herd a flock (or a rancher trying to control a stampede!).

Most babies begin to walk between twelve and fifteen months, but the process can start as early as nine months or as late as eighteen months. Keep in mind that many multiples that were born early have an adjusted timetable for development, and may walk later. As with other milestones, your doctor will offer guidance on the appropriate rate of development for your individual children. Your multiples may have different levels of readiness and ability and several weeks or even months may pass between first steps.

After they can walk, your twins may discover another fun skill: climbing. Most parents of multiples will confirm that a team of toddlers are much more adept at feats of climbing than any single child. Don't ever underestimate your multiples' ability to outwit any attempts to defeat their drive to scale higher heights.

Taking twins or multiples out in public can become a frightening prospect at this age, especially for parents who have more children than hands. Keeping track of one child is difficult enough; they

Mindful Mommy

Many families find it necessary to temporarily dismantle their home, barricading bookshelves, removing dining room chairs to keep twins off the table, and anchoring dressers to the wall to prevent them from toppling onto toddlers.

can dart off in the blink of an eye. Keeping track of multiples is trickier; if one darts off, do you give chase and leave the other(s) to her own devices? That's one reason that a good stroller is a worthy investment for parents of multiples. It's an ideal way to keep their kids close at hand in public situations, and many parents find that they use it more often and longer for multiples than they would for a single child.

Another controversial option is the use of leashes or safety harnesses. They attach to a child's wrist or torso on one end, while mom or dad takes hold of the other end. Some are even designed especially for multiples, with multiple belts connected to a single clip. They're not for everyone; some families are uncomfortable with the extra attention they attract, and argue that children shouldn't be treated like pets. But many parents of multiples disagree, appreciating the combination of security and freedom they provide. They let toddlers roam, yet allow parents to keep them close at hand.

Talking Times Two

Not only do they walk the walk, but now they talk the talk. From coos and gurgles emerged the early babbling sounds of "mama," "dada," and "baba." Around the time of their first birthday, most children will understand several words and some will even say a few, although not particularly clearly. Over the course of the second year, most will experience an explosion of vocabulary, stringing together words to form simple sentences and able to understand and respond to a great deal of what's said to them.

Many twins and multiples will experience delays in speech development. There is a general assumption that babies born prematurely or with a low birth weight lag behind, and many multiples fall into this category. But even full-term, healthy twins can exhibit language delays. Is it simply because they are multiples?

Researchers have offered several explanations. It's an unfortunate fact that parents of multiples simply have less time for one-on-one interaction with their babies. Twins receive less directed speech from their parents than singleton babies. Babies learn, not only by mimicking your speech, but also by the feedback you provide in response to their vocalizations.

Some multiples experience speech delays because they rely on other modes of communicating, including with each other. For example, they may point or grunt instead of vocalizing the sound for "cup" when they are thirsty. Busy parents of multiples don't always have the time or patience to reverse this trend, especially when two or more babies are clamoring for cups. But make the effort to encourage them to use the correct word or phrase, and then praise their efforts at communication.

Another assumption about twins is that they share a secret, made-up language that only they can understand. While that could explain a lag in their language ability, the concept of *idioglossia*—or twin

talk—is generally a fascinating idea rather than an actuality or a cause for concern. Some twins may appear to speak in their own secret language, but it's more likely that they are simply mimicking each other's incoherent or incorrect speech patterns. It's possible they do actually understand each other, and it's certainly cute, but it's more important to encourage healthy speech development so that they'll be understood by everyone.

Toddler twins can get quite ingenious at finding ways to communicate. Unfortunately, one of their most common—and frustrating—attempts is using their mouth in the wrong way, by biting. Frequently, the unhappy recipient of their attempts is their co-twin. Biting can be a big problem for twins and multiples, if it's not nipped in the bud. (Pardon the pun!)

If one of your multiples is biting, the best approach is to tell them firmly, "No biting!" and remove them from the situation. Some parents employ other techniques, finding it effective to endow positive attention on the bitten child, give the biter a taste of his own medicine, or use distraction to diffuse the situation. Ultimately, the most important tactic is to be consistent in your response to a biting situation.

Mommy Must

It's important to talk interactively to your babies at every opportunity. It's never too early or too often, and it doesn't matter too much what you say. Rather, it's the sound of your voice, the exposure to new words and phrases, as well as your facial expression in response to their attempts at communication.

If you're concerned about your multiples' lags in language, contact your doctor. Early intervention programs may be available to provide the therapy that will enable your multiples to catch up to their singleton peers.

Mommies of Multiples Do:
- Make an extra effort to overcome language delay by talking to their babies as well as responding to their attempts at communication.
- Seek evaluation and early intervention, if necessary, if their children experience the speech and language issues common to multiples.

Mommies of Multiples Don't:
- Allow one twin or multiple to do all the talking for another; instead encourage each child to develop his/her language skills.
- Ignore toddlers who use biting or hitting in place of verbal communication.
- Let "twin talk" replace normal patterns of speech.

When to Wean?

When your babies were newborns, your main activity was feeding them around the clock, nursing or bottle-feeding every few hours. It's hard to believe, but the time is approaching to wean them away from their liquid diet. As you've introduced solid foods, they've obtained less and less of their daily nutrition from breast milk or formula. By the time of their first birthday, solid foods compose the majority of their diet.

Weaning from breastfeeding is a personal issue and will be different for every mother and every child, even for multiples. Although your babies no longer rely solely on breast milk to sustain them nutritionally, there are many physical and emotional benefits to extended nursing. With multiples, one of the key advantages is an opportunity for bonding between a mother and child. You may be hesitant to give up that special time with each of your babies.

Weaning is a process, and it may take place over the course of several weeks or months. It usually evolves as a series of gradual changes in your nursing routine, but it also can come about rather abruptly due to an illness or other circumstances. As the mother of your multiples, you are in the best position to determine the right time to wean.

Mindful Mommy

In the United States, the American Academy of Pediatricians recommends breastfeeding for twelve months, but in other countries it is not uncommon to nurse a baby for two or more years. Many babies are ready to wean between twelve and eighteen months of age.

Making Your Home a Safe Haven

If you have other children, you probably already have safeguards in place throughout your home. However, there are some extra precautionary measures to consider when you have twins or more. You've probably heard the old saying, "Two heads are better than one." Well, when it comes to outwitting parents' efforts to keep them out of trouble, that phrase is all too true about twin toddlers. Not only are there four hands for reaching and pulling, and four feet for climbing and running, but a twosome is always more creatively daring than one child on his own. And if two can wreak more havoc than one, just imagine what destruction three, four, or more can create!

You can't possibly anticipate every single danger or risk in your home. But you can try to minimize the potential for accidents or damage, both to your precious children and to your home's contents! Here are some general tips for making your home a safe haven.

Mommies of Multiples Do:
- Store anything breakable or irreplaceable. There's always time for knickknacks when their multiples are grown.
- Keep their kids close to the ground. Eliminate any situation that can create stair steps; secure dresser drawers, shelves, even dining room chairs.

- Beat the heat. Lower the setting on their hot water heater and install anti-scald devices on their faucets to prevent burns.
- Accessorize their appliances. Consider child safety devices that prevent access to the dishwasher, refrigerator, toilet, or oven.
- Watch the windows. Window guards will prevent accidental falls. Be sure to use products that are easily removed by adults if window access is necessary in the event of an emergency.
- Think about blinds and other window treatments. They could present a strangulation hazard. Keep cords short and inaccessible, or use cord stops to keep cords contained.
- Designate a safe zone—a place within their home that can be secured and freed of all possible hazards.
- Maintain their smoke detectors and carbon monoxide detectors to keep them in working order and create an evacuation plan for their home in the event of a fire.
- Keep important phone numbers handy in multiple locations throughout the house, including the number for poison control.

Mommies of Multiples Don't:
- Keep any toxic chemicals, such as cleaning products or paints, within reach. Be sure the storage location has a lock or other obstacle.

- Leave sharp edges exposed. Bumpers or pillows can help soften the blow, but why not remove furniture with sharp corners altogether?
- Leave stair access and banister railings unprotected. Don't neglect to block off the bottom as well, to keep kids from climbing up and falling back down.
- Expose your electronics. Plastic guards keep prying fingers from sensitive areas of your television, stereo, computer, or other electronic equipment.

These changes to your home are temporary and worthwhile. At times, you may feel that you've been the victim of a home invasion and that it has been overtaken by twin "stuff." Remember, this isn't a lifestyle that you'll have to cope with forever.

Becoming Individuals

It's fascinating to watch individual personalities emerge as your multiples mature. Although you've probably observed unique qualities in them from birth, the details of their individual personalities are coming into focus as they approach toddlerhood. They adopt their own preferences, express their personal emotions, and establish unique habits. For some multiples, particularly monozygotics, their similarities become more pronounced, but often it is the differences that are most apparent.

As a parent of multiples, you are tasked with a unique responsibility: to nurture your children as individuals, but also to encourage their bond and celebrate their status as multiples. It's part of who they are, but it's not all there is to them. It can be challenging to help them find their way as individuals when the rest of society wants to lump them together, picking apart every detail and holding them up for comparison.

There are some basic attitudes and strategies that will help you encourage their individuality, and it's never too early to adopt them as part of your parenting philosophy. Let them be who they are. Don't apply labels and expect them to conform to your expectations. Some people feel that birth order should define personality, that the first-born multiple will adopt the typical leadership characteristics of a first-born child, while the last-born will take on the role of the baby of the family. However, those assumptions don't hold true for multiples. Others tend to use comparative terms to distinguish twins: good twin/bad twin, easygoing/fussy, leader/follower. Try to avoid these kinds of comparisons in your own attitudes and extinguish them when you hear others applying them to your children.

If your twins or multiples are monozygotic and have a similar physical appearance, it can be difficult to tell them apart, especially for those outside your immediate family. But it's important for children to be acknowledged as individuals, so make it a priority to distinguish them wherever possible. Make it easier for teachers, day care providers, neighbors, and friends to tell them apart by referring to them by name or by providing clues to their identity. For example, introduce them with a color code. "Here is Johnny, in blue, and this is Jimmy, in green." Others will appreciate your assistance, and your multiples benefit, too. Adult twins often report that one of their pet peeves growing up was being referred to as "the twins" instead of being recognized by name.

Finally, it's never too early to spend one-on-one time with each child. Although time is at a premium when you're a mother of young multiples, don't miss out on this important bonding opportunity. Carve out time in your day, perhaps before bedtime, during a bath, or while feeding individually, to devote some uninterrupted one-on-one interaction to each child. Or, integrate these opportunities into your weekly routine, making them a tradition so that each parent has an opportunity to spend time alone with a child. Perhaps one twin could accompany dad on Saturday morning errands. Or one triplet joins mom in the yard for thirty minutes of weeding. However you fit it in, these one-on-one times will become a cherished tradition for parents as well as children.

Their First Birthday—a Celebration of Them . . . And You!

It's hard to believe, but an era is coming to a close . . . the first year of your twins' or multiples' lives. It's a time for celebration, for them, and for you! They've come a long way since their first days as tiny infants, while you've become quite adept at caring for them. You've grown as a family and their first birthday should be a celebration of all that you've accomplished together.

One thing that multiples will always share is a birthday, and thus it's a particularly special day for them. As you prepare to celebrate their first birthday, give some thought to how you can make it special and unique. This is your chance to establish traditions that will be carried forward in the years to come. Here are some things to consider:

Cake: Will you have one cake to share, or give each child their own? Cupcakes are an ideal solution to this dilemma, especially for toddlers who are mostly interested in smooshing it into their hair.

Singing "Happy Birthday": One for all, or all for one? Some families sing a single song for the group, while others elect to sing it multiple times, to give each child their own special serenade.

Presents: One present for each, or one gift for them to share? Gift-giving for multiples is an ongoing source of confusion and consternation. It's not a bad idea to think about your preferences and set a precedent to avoid any hurt feelings. There are many approaches to the issue. If every guest brings a gift for every multiple, your home could soon be overrun with toys! Some people prefer to give party guests a polite suggestion, perhaps that female guests bring a gift for the girl twin while male guests provide for the boy.

As you prepare to celebrate their first birthday, give some thought to establishing a special tradition that you can carry out for all the years to come. Perhaps you'll have their photograph made in the same spot every year, so that you can track their growth. Write them each a letter to document all the special events of the past year. Plan an outing to a favorite place like a park, the zoo, or a museum that the entire family can enjoy year after year.

Some families elect to celebrate their multiples' birthdays separately, so that they can enjoy individual festivities. They may schedule them on consecutive days, or scatter the celebrations throughout the year. Another tradition to consider is how you will enable your multiples to celebrate each other on their birthday. Will they exchange gifts? Make cards for each other when they're old enough to be creative?

Mindful Mommy

Many families find it less stressful to open gifts after the party is over, especially when there are duplicate gifts. For older multiples, much of the enjoyment of anticipating a gift is ruined when their co-twin already has an identical present, and opening gifts in private can soften hurt feelings.

The Challenges Ahead

"When does it get easier?" is the lament of many a mom. Some consider the first year with multiples to be the toughest. But there are still many challenges to come.

So, let's look at some of the special challenges you'll face as a parent of twins or multiples. Just ahead on the horizon is potty training. It may seem hard to imagine a day when you won't be changing multiple diapers, but it will come. Don't be too eager, however. If your multiples aren't ready, the only result of your efforts will be frustration. It's quite possible that your multiples won't be ready at the same time; often girls show an interest and signs of readiness long before their brothers. Work with each child individually, and you'll likely see that one's success encourages the progress of the other.

Further down the road, a day will come when your multiples start school. You may have to face some decisions about their classroom placement. For some twins, it's best to keep them together, in the same classroom. Other multiples benefit from being

Mommy Must

Everyone needs their own potty. Plan to have one on hand for each child. Chances are when one has to go, the other will want a turn as well.

separated. In some cases, the decision will be made for you, for example, in a school with a single class per grade. Some families encounter a great deal of opposition from their school's administration, which doesn't always welcome parental input into place- ment decisions. Take the time to fully research the issue; talk to other parents of multiples in your school system as well as the professionals, like a pediatrician, preschool teacher, or day care provider, who know your children best.

As your multiples grow up, they'll have the advantage of being part of a pair, or a team, enjoying the support and friendship of their co-multiples. But they'll also contend with some issues unique to being a multiple: intense rivalry and competition, constant comparison against their twin, and a struggle to cre- ate their own identity. As a parent, it will be your job to guide them through these issues. You won't always have all the answers, but you can equip them with the tools to resolve their problems and find their own way in the world.

Chapter 11

Finding the Support
You Need

HAVING MULTIPLES IS MUCH more manageable when you take a team approach. You simply can't do it alone. Assistance comes in a variety of forms: professional services, neighbors and friends, babysitters, medical advisers, or family members. Figuring out what kind of help will be most beneficial is half the battle.

There Are Other
Moms Just Like You!

One of the first things you should do upon discovering that you are having twins, triplets, or more is to develop a support group of families in similar circumstances. Talking to parents who have been through the experience will not only prove reassuring, but will help you prepare to face the challenges ahead. Luckily for parents of multiples, a vast network of fellow families exists throughout the world.

You'll find multiples clubs and parenting organizations in nearly every region of the United States, and in most countries of the world.

These groups evolved in recognition of the tremendous benefit of sharing support and advice among fellow families of twins and other multiples. Parents of multiples face unique challenges that parents of singletons don't understand. They have much to gain from the experience of others.

The Benefits of Belonging

In the United States, the NOMOTC is a network of nearly 500 clubs, representing over 20,000 individual families. Most NOMOTC-affiliated clubs offer monthly meetings, programs about parenting multiples, resource libraries, and clothing/equipment sales. Some groups are large and busy, while others are small and casual. Other opportunities that the clubs might offer include

- Playgroups organized by community or multiples' ages
- Meal delivery for families with newborns
- Outings for moms or couples

Mommy Knows Best

The National Organization of Mothers of Twins Clubs (NOMOTC) is a nonprofit organization founded in 1960 to promote the special aspects of child development that relate specifically to multiple birth children. To find a club in your area, call the NOMOTC (877-243-2276) or stop by their Web site at *www.nomotc.org*.

- Babysitting co-op
- Monthly newsletter
- Family activities such as picnics or visits to theme parks
- Mentor or buddy programs for expectant mothers
- Community discount program
- Service opportunities benefiting the community or needy families
- Regional and national conferences with speakers, discussion forums, and classes about parenting multiples

Membership in a local organization gives you the additional benefit of national membership. In addition to NOMOTC affiliates, there are numerous independent clubs. If you are having difficulty locating a club in your area, inquire through your physician or hospital; they can usually put you in touch with someone.

Usually, families that are expecting multiples or have newborns are invited to visit a monthly meeting without obligation. If you decide to join, there is usually a membership fee to become a member and take advantage of the club's benefits. Part of the fee

Mindful Mommy

Even if you don't like to commit to committees, it's worth investigating the multiples organization in your area. You can usually visit a meeting or talk by phone with a club representative before making a commitment. These organizations exist to serve parents, not obligate them, so don't worry that you'll be expected to participate in anything you're uncomfortable with.

will be designated for the national and regional club, while the remainder is used to fund the local club's activities.

Who Belongs?

Club designations vary. Some are called "parents of multiples clubs" while others specify "mothers of twins." In reality, the majority of programming and support is generally aimed at the mother, although some clubs include grandparents, adopted parents, and caregivers of multiples.

Some larger cities have a designated group for families with triplets, quadruplets, or higher order multiples. If your area does not offer such a group, two national organizations may offer some support. The Triplet Connection offers information packets and presents an annual conference. Membership in MOST (Mothers of Supertwins) entitles you to receive phone support, access to online resources, and a quarterly magazine. (Contact information for both groups can be found in Appendix A.)

Online Groups Can Guide You Too

The Internet has opened up a whole new world for parents of multiples. Up-to-date information is readily available from the comfort of your living room at any time of the day or night. In addition, you can enjoy immediate access to fellow parents from

around the world without worrying about jet lag or even whether you've had time to shower that day.

Although books like this one are invaluable collections of resources and facts, the Internet has the added benefit of providing up-to-the-minute updates about multiple birth issues, including crucial medical advances. If you encounter a specific problem in your pregnancy, such as twin-to-twin transfusion syndrome, or are fighting the battle against preterm labor, you can research in-depth explanations about possible treatments and options.

In addition to factual information, the Internet is a tremendous human resource. You've already learned that fellow parents are your best source of advice, and the Internet puts that font of wisdom literally at your fingertips. You can connect with other parents via chats, discussion forums, message boards, e-mail, and instant messaging. You can communicate as part of a group or one-on-one with individuals.

The Welcoming Web

So how do you find fellow parents online? Start at Web sites focused on the topic of parenting multiples; many have community features that connect

Mommy Must

Be sure to discuss any medical information you find on the Internet with your doctor. Just because something is published online doesn't ensure that it is accurate, or appropriate, for your individual circumstances.

users via chats or message boards. Chats are scheduled events, bringing together individual users at a designated time in an online chat room where they can participate in real-time interactive discussions. Message boards—also called discussion boards or forums—are ongoing discussions where users add their comments and responses in the form of posts.

Online mailing lists about multiple birth allow families to communicate via e-mail. Some lists take the form of informational newsletters, while others are more interactive in nature. If you have inquiries about a specific topic or desire the ability to respond to comments, you'll want to subscribe to the latter.

Online communication has many benefits for families with multiples. First, it's available when you are, twenty-four hours a day and seven days a week. When you have newborn twins, triplets, or more in the house, you can't keep banker's hours. You may be asleep from 9 A.M. until noon, and wide awake at 3 A.M. Using e-mail or other online communication tools allows you to keep in touch with people according to your schedule. If you find a few free minutes while the babies nap, you can go online and accomplish several tasks that would take hours to do offline: share photos, pay bills, shop, find a recipe for dinner,

Mindful Mommy

Look for venues that are moderated to keep things clean. In addition, choose forums with plenty of recent responses so that you know someone is paying attention and there is enough traffic to sustain conversation.

get information on baby care, network with other parents, send out e-mail updates about the babies' progress, and more!

Several online resources are included in Appendix A. Spend some time browsing to discover a world of information about twins and multiples, including medical resources, parenting advice, multiple-themed merchandise, online communities, and much more. A word of caution is in order, however. Just as in the "real" world, the virtual world has its share of hazards. Be wary of people you encounter online. Identity falsification is rampant; it's difficult to confirm that the person on your computer screen is who they claim to be. Use common sense: don't send money to, agree to meet with, or become emotionally invested in anyone you meet online without checking out their credentials.

Back to Class

One of the most stereotypical traditions of pregnancy is attending a childbirth class with your partner. You lie on pillows on the floor, practice funny breathing, and dreamily anticipate the joy of welcoming your new baby. Unfortunately, the reality of these classes is that they are not always relevant to the multiple birth experience. Preterm labor or bed rest may prohibit you from making it to a class if you wait until the third trimester. A scheduled c-section would eliminate the need for labor management instruction. However, childbirth preparation classes aren't entirely a waste of time for parents of multiples. There are several ways that you can derive benefit from formal instruction.

What to Expect

First-time parents are usually the most common candidates for childbirth education. If your multiples will be your first born—as well as second, and maybe third—then you should definitely consider a class that covers the basics of labor and delivery. Some of the things that might be covered are

- Different methods of labor management, such as Bradley or Lamaze
- Explanation of the stages of labor
- Anesthesia and medication
- Complications
- Relaxation and pain management

Some classes also address the mother's postpartum care, newborn care, cesarean birth procedures,

Mommy Knows Best

You may find it helpful to team up with one or two other couples who are also having twins or more and enroll in a class together. That way, you're not the exception in the class. Don't be afraid to inform the instructor about your multiple pregnancy, and inquire as to how each topic relates to a multiple birth.

or the father's role. If you've experienced a previous pregnancy and normal delivery, you may find that this type of beginner class is redundant. You may be more interested in a refresher class, VBAC (vaginal birth after cesarean) preparation, sibling adjustment training, or other programs for veteran parents.

Information about childbirth education is usually available from your doctor or hospital. It can be helpful to take a class at the hospital where you plan to deliver the babies because policies and procedures often vary from one location to the next. You may also have the opportunity to tour your hospital's maternity and nursery departments so that you are familiar with the facilities.

Most singleton families wait until the third trimester to enroll in birthing classes, but parents of multiples are advised not to put it off! If you are expecting twins, you should plan to complete your class before the end of your second trimester. If you are expecting triplets or more, the end of the first trimester is not too early to begin your training. Preterm labor or bed rest restrictions may preclude you from attending later in the pregnancy.

Mindful Mommy

Marvelous Multiples recommends that mothers attend a class before their twenty-second week of pregnancy, in order to gain the maximum benefit from the information.

Multiple-Specific Classes

In recent years, as the number of multiple births has increased, greater attention has been focused on the unique circumstances of parents of multiples. Fortunately, that has resulted in more opportunities for multiple birth families to receive education specific to their situation. Classes on managing multiple pregnancy, labor and delivery with multiples, and newborn care of multiples are becoming more readily available.

Marvelous Multiples is a national network of classes designed for parents of multiples. Classes are available in most states in the United States as well as throughout Canada. Going beyond childbirth education, it covers many vital topics about multiples including

- Physical and emotional challenges of multiple pregnancy
- Variances in labor, delivery, and recovery with multiples
- Newborn care of multiples
- Networking with other families

Some programs are sponsored by a nonprofit organization and are available for free. Others charge a fee. Some of the costs may be offset by your insurance coverage. Many of the programs are associated with hospitals or local mothers of multiples clubs, either of which can provide full details regarding class schedules and registration. You can also check

Marvelous Multiples' Web site (*www.marvelousmul tiples.com*) for class locations.

Enlist Your Family and Friends

Many families with multiples are fortunate to find themselves the beneficiaries of numerous offers of assistance from friends and relatives. Some even have the support of an entire neighborhood or church community. However, just because help is available doesn't mean that it is helpful. You'll want to be sure that you accept help in ways that make life with multiples easier, not more complicated.

Help During Pregnancy

There are many instances throughout a multiple pregnancy when you can use a bit of assistance. Because mothers of multiples experience more complications, they may find themselves restricted to bed or hospitalized at some point during their pregnancy. To a lesser extreme, they may simply find that their physical symptoms are intensified to the point where normal activities become uncomfortable and everyday chores and responsibilities may become a burden. During those times, it's very helpful to have some assistance lined up, such as meal preparation, errand running, or child care for older siblings.

It can also be a very emotional time, with lots of anxiety about what lies ahead. Pregnancy is a good time to call upon friends for reassurance and encouragement. See a funny movie or laugh about old times together. A mother's emotional state has a great deal of influence over her physical condition; friends can play an important role in keeping her spirits uplifted.

Help after the Babies Come Home

Once your babies arrive and your family's focus shifts to round-the-clock newborn nurturing, opportunities abound for outside assistance. Don't be afraid to accept help, and don't hesitate to ask for it, either. People genuinely want to help, and you genuinely need it. Take everyone up on their offers, but utilize the help in such a way that it serves your needs.

First, be specific about what you need. Nearly everyone wants to "help" by holding or rocking a baby. Sometimes that's nice if it offers you a break to accomplish something else, but be realistic about how helpful it really is. Do you need help finishing chores? Or caring for other children? Some families with higher order multiples may require help around the clock, just to get all the babies fed and changed!

Some other forms of assistance you might want to consider are:

Mommy Must

Tiny newborns, especially if they were preterm, are particularly susceptible to dangerous infections due to underdeveloped immunity. Explain proper hand-washing techniques to your helpers, and enforce a policy that requires them to wash up before touching the babies.

- Extra hands at feeding times
- Telephone answering and filtering calls
- Photography
- Meals for the family
- Laundry
- Yard work
- Errand running
- Transportation
- Bathtime assistance
- Care for other siblings (homework help, playtime)

Once you have established your needs, organize your helpers. Preferably have someone else organize the help. The less you have to worry about anything other than the babies, the better. An efficient organizer is the best helper you can have. Have her create a list of your needs, then match helpers according to their abilities and availabilities.

Helpers will appreciate having a specified opportunity to help. For example, saying, "Please come by at 7 p.m. on Thursday to help feed the babies and put them to bed" lets your friends know exactly what is expected of them. It allows you to receive help at the times you need it most, while discouraging unwelcome drop-in visitors when you're sleeping or otherwise occupied.

Try to determine ahead of time when you will need the most assistance. Most families find that they require the majority of help in the first few weeks after their babies are born and/or when they bring them home. Fortunately, that's usually when the most offers for help are made. After a few months, the need for help diminishes somewhat as the family adjusts and establishes a routine. However, you may find that you would appreciate some form of ongoing or occasional assistance for several months longer, perhaps a weekly meal delivery, occasional babysitting so that Mom and Dad can enjoy a night out (or in!), or transportation to the babies' three-month checkup with the pediatrician.

But I Don't Want Help

If you are very independent—or very organized—you may not wish to have your home and private family life invaded by outsiders. That's okay, too. Don't refuse all offers of help outright, however. Instead, specify ways that meet your needs while respecting your privacy and comfort level. Perhaps you would find it helpful to have a friend pick up some items at the grocery store rather than prepare a meal. Or maybe you'd prefer for your mother-in-law to help care for your older children rather than the new babies. Make a mental note of the friends and family members who offer their help so that you can call on

Mindful Mommy

Ongoing or occasional cleaning assistance makes a great gift for new parents. If you're making up a wish list, go ahead and include it! Because of the cost, a group of gift-givers may wish to combine their resources and present the gift together.

them down the road if you do find yourself in need at a later time.

Professional Help, at Your Service

Sometimes volunteer help simply isn't enough. There are times when you'll need to call in a professional. If you can afford to pay for help, you may find it well worth the cost. Decide how your money will be best spent by considering what services you can turn over to another party while you concentrate on the activities that mean the most to you.

Help Around the House

When multiples join a household, things change forever. If you've been accustomed to cleaning and maintaining your home, you may find that your time to devote to it is severely diminished once your babies arrive. While housework still needs to be done, it is one of the responsibilities that most people don't mind giving up. Paying for a cleaning service to maintain your home removes the burden and lets you focus your attention on your new babies. Even if you don't need ongoing service, a one-time thorough cleaning would help you put your home in order and get your expanded family off to a good start.

In addition to housekeeping, there are several other home responsibilities that can be turned over to professionals in order to free up expectant or new parents' time. For example, meal preparation services are becoming very popular options for busy families. Professional landscapers can take over yard work duties. Pet sitters can relieve you of pet chores such as feeding, walking, and cleaning up. Professional organizers can help you streamline your routines and reduce clutter in your home to make your lifestyle more efficient.

Help with the Babies

Professional advice and assistance with caring for your newborn multiples can literally be a lifesaver. First-time parents, parents of premature multiples, or parents of infants with special medical needs will greatly benefit from the personal attention of a hired nurse or caregiver, such as a doula.

Doulas provide a comforting, supportive presence to mothers—and fathers—during childbirth, but are also available for postpartum care. As an objective and neutral party, they act as an advocate for the family and an intermediary between the parents and the medical staff. Postpartum doulas assist the mother with breastfeeding, recuperation from delivery, and newborn care. Most postpartum doulas charge by

Mindful Mommy

Few families require around-the-clock care, but many find it useful to have an occasional visit from a postpartum doula or nurse. Your insurance may help cover the costs of these services, so be sure to investigate your options before ruling it out.

the hour, so you have the option of procuring as little or as much service as you require. Even a one-hour visit with a postpartum doula can boost new parents' confidence and provide valuable information about caring for their newborns. A short-term investment in professional help may assist you in becoming better parents in the long run.

With sleep deprivation an issue for so many new parents of multiples, the promise of a good night's sleep may be worth the cost of hiring a night nurse—a professional nurse who will come to your home to care for the babies throughout the nighttime hours so you and your partner can sleep. Costs vary, but even one night of uninterrupted sleep can improve parents' perspective and equip them to cope with their babies going forward.

Counseling Services

Finally, don't overlook your mental health as you adjust to your newly expanded family. Having twins or multiples can be extremely stressful. It may prove tremendously helpful to find someone to talk to about your feelings. For some individuals, talking to a friend, relative, or fellow parent may be sufficient. Others, however, may require psychological support from a professional. Families who experience any of the following would be good candidates for professional counseling:

- Complicated pregnancy with high levels of stress or anxiety

- Loss of a twin or multiple
- Preterm labor resulting in premature or ill babies
- Selective reduction
- Postpartum depression
- Trouble adjusting to the demands of caring for multiple babies
- Marital problems

Serious consequences, including depression or divorce, can result if you let your emotional issues remain unresolved. Parents often neglect their own needs in their efforts to care for their children, but receiving support from a counselor or psychologist can only enhance your parenting. Your doctor or your local multiples club can steer you toward professionals who have experience helping new parents and families with multiples.

Resources, Additional Readings, Online Help

Additional Reading

Agnew, Connie L., Klein, Alan H., and Ganon, Jill Alison. *Twins! Pregnancy, Birth and the First Year of Life* (HarperCollins, 2006)

Gromada, Karen Kerkhoff. *Mothering Multiples: Breastfeeding and Caring for Twins or More* (La Leche League International, 2007)

Hanselman, Jennifer. *Party of Nine: The Triumphs and Traumas of Raising Sextuplets + One* (Saddle Point, 2006)

Heim, Susan M. *Twice the Love: Stories of Inspiration for Families . . . with Twins, Multiples, and Singletons* (Twins Magazine, 2006)

Kohl, Susan. *Twin Stories: Their Mysterious and Unique Bond* (Wildcat Canyon Press, 2001)

Lage, Cheryl. *Twinspiration: Real-Life Advice From Pregnancy Through the First Year for Parents of Twins and Multiples* (Taylor Trade Publishing, 2007)

Luke, Barbara. *Every Pregnant Woman's Guide to Preventing Preterm Labor* (Author's Choice Press, 2002)

Luke, Barbara and Eberlein, Tamara. *When You're Expecting Twins, Triplets or More* (Perennial, 2004)

Lyons, Elizabeth. *Ready or Not, Here We Come! The Real Experts' Cannot-Live-Without Guide to the First Year with Twins* (Finn-Phyllis Press, 2003)

Lyons, Elizabeth. *Ready or Not . . . There We Go! The REAL Experts' Guide to the Toddler Years with Twins* (Finn-Phyllis Press, 2006)

Moskwinski, Rebecca E. (Ed.) *Twins to Quints: The Complete Manual for Parents of Multiple Birth Children* (Harpeth House Publishing, 2002)

Noble, Elizabeth. *Having Twins and More* (Houghton Mifflin, 2003)

Sipes, Nancy J. and Sipes, Janna S. *Dancing Naked in Front of the Fridge and Other Lessons from Twins* (FairWinds Press, 1998)

Tinglof, Christina Baglivi. *Parenting School-Age Twins and Multiples* (McGraw-Hill, 2006)

Twins Magazine (Published six times a year.)
888-55-TWINS or 303-290-8500
twins.customer.service@businessword.com
www.twinsmagazine.com

Online Resources

General Information on Multiples
Guide to Parenting Multiples at About.com
multiples.guide@about.com
www.multiples.about.com

Twinstuff.com
www.twinstuff.com

Multiple Birth: Prenatal Education and Bereavement Support
www.multiplebirthsfamilies.com

Twins-L Listserve
www.twinslist.org

Clubs for Parents of Multiples
National Organization of Mothers of Twins Clubs (NOMOTC)
P.O. Box 438
Thompson Station, TN 37179-0438
877-243-2276
info@nomotc.org, www.nomotc.org

Multiple Births Canada
P.O. Box 432
Wasaga Beach, Ontario
Canada L0L 2P0
705-429-0901
office@multiplebirthscanada.org
www.multiplebirthscanada.org

Pregnancy and Breastfeeding Support
Doulas of North America (DONA)
P.O. Box 626
Jasper, IN 47547
888-788-DONA
referrals@dona.org
www.dona.org

Marvelous Multiples
Nancy Bowers, RN
P.O. Box 381164
Birmingham, AL 35238
205-437-3575
marvmult@aol.com
www.marvelousmultiples.com

Sidelines Pregnancy Support
P.O. Box 1808
Laguna Beach, CA 92652
888-447-4754 or 949-497-5598
sidelines@sidelines.org
www.sidelines.org

La Leche League International
1400 N. Meacham Road
Schamburg, IL 60173-4808
847-519-7730 or 800-LALECHE
www.lalecheleague.org

Medela, Inc.
1101 Corporate Drive
McHenry, IL 60050
800-435-8316 or 815-363-1166
customer.service@medela.com
www.medela.com

Higher Order Multiples
Mothers of Supertwins (MOST)
P.O. Box 951
Brentwood, NY 11717
631-859-1110
info@MOSTonline.org
www.mostonline.org

Triplet Connection
Janet Bleyl, President
P.O. Box 693392
Stockton, CA 95269-3392
209-474-0885
janet@tripletconnection.org
www.tripletconnection.org

Keeping Track: Charting Your Newborns' Progress

Use this chart to help you keep track of your babies' feedings, diaper activity, and administration of any medications each day. This form will accommodate up to four babies; print out two per day if you have quintuplets or higher.

Filling Out Your Progress Chart

At the top of each column, note the babies' names. Each time you feed and change the babies, note the time in the left-hand column. Under each baby's name, fill in the four squares.

Feed: Indicate the amount of formula in ounces, or the amount of time spent breastfeeding in minutes. If breastfeeding, you may also wish to indicate which breast the baby nursed from, with an "R" to designate the right side and an "L" for the left side.

Med: If any of your babies require medications, you can use this space to keep track of the dosages. Check the box when you have administered medication to make sure that each baby is getting the right dose at the right time.

WD: Use this space to record the number of wet diapers since the last feeding. It's important that each baby is urinating enough to soak a diaper. A lack of wet diapers could indicate dehydration.

BM: This section also represents your baby's diaper achievements. Use it to record bowel movements. You can use a tally system or just check the box after you've changed a soiled diaper.

Today's Date _____

	Baby A:		Baby B:	
Time	Feed:	Med:	Feed:	Med:
	WD:	BM:	WD:	BM:
Time	Feed:	Med:	Feed:	Med:
	WD:	BM:	WD:	BM:
Time	Feed:	Med:	Feed:	Med:
	WD:	BM:	WD:	BM:
Time	Feed:	Med:	Feed:	Med:
	WD:	BM:	WD:	BM:
Time	Feed:	Med:	Feed:	Med:
	WD:	BM:	WD:	BM:
Time	Feed:	Med:	Feed:	Med:
	WD:	BM:	WD:	BM:
Time	Feed:	Med:	Feed:	Med:
	WD:	BM:	WD:	BM:
Time	Feed:	Med:	Feed:	Med:
	WD:	BM:	WD:	BM:
Time	Feed:	Med:	Feed:	Med:
	WD:	BM:	WD:	BM:
Time	Feed:	Med:	Feed:	Med:
	WD:	BM:	WD:	BM:

Today's Date _____

	Baby C:		Baby D:	
Time	Feed:	Med:	Feed:	Med:
	WD:	BM:	WD:	BM:
Time	Feed:	Med:	Feed:	Med:
	WD:	BM:	WD:	BM:
Time	Feed:	Med:	Feed:	Med:
	WD:	BM:	WD:	BM:
Time	Feed:	Med:	Feed:	Med:
	WD:	BM:	WD:	BM:
Time	Feed:	Med:	Feed:	Med:
	WD:	BM:	WD:	BM:
Time	Feed:	Med:	Feed:	Med:
	WD:	BM:	WD:	BM:
Time	Feed:	Med:	Feed:	Med:
	WD:	BM:	WD:	BM:
Time	Feed:	Med:	Feed:	Med:
	WD:	BM:	WD:	BM:
Time	Feed:	Med:	Feed:	Med:
	WD:	BM:	WD:	BM:
Time	Feed:	Med:	Feed:	Med:
	WD:	BM:	WD:	BM:

Index